A STUDENT IN THE SCHOOL OF CHRIST

Wasihun Senbeta Gutema

WESTBOW
PRESS®
A DIVISION OF THOMAS NELSON
& ZONDERVAN

WestBow Press books may be ordered through booksellers or by contacting:

WestBow Press
A Division of Thomas Nelson & Zondervan
1663 Liberty Drive
Bloomington, IN 47403
www.westbowpress.com
844-714-3454

All Scripture quotations are taken from The Holy Bible, New International Version®, NIV® Copyright © 1973, 1978, 1984, 2011 by Biblica, Inc.® Used by permission. All rights reserved worldwide.

ISBN: 978-1-6642-4306-4 (sc)
ISBN: 978-1-6642-4304-0 (hc)
ISBN: 978-1-6642-4305-7 (e)

Library of Congress Control Number: 2021916923

Print information available on the last page.

WestBow Press rev. date: 10/25/2021

Note for the Readers

Student and disciple or disciples are used
together or interchangeably
Studentship or discipleship are used together or interchangeably

Contents

Preface

This book presents a revision of my teachings in the local congregations. It also presents my immense readings, my passion to be a true student of Christ and my prayer to see the followers of Christ to be true students/disciples of the Lord Jesus Christ. Three factors captured my fascination about the Students/ Disciples of Christ. Jesus called students/disciples and no more or less. He called His disciples to follow Him learning His words, thus followers and learners. First, it is apparent that Jesus called all of us to be His disciples/ students and what it constitutes – a repudiation of belongings, a renunciation of the matters that drag us and a measure to take irreversible action prioritizing Christ.

The second factor that captured me was whether Jesus called Christians or students. True Christians are always the students of Christ. They are learners, humble and always witness and live Christ as their Master. There was no other call than a call to be a student. There was no other alternative to which we are called as believers. It was and is to be students and the students of Christ have no room for anything other than living Christ. They are called to live for Christ regardless of time and space. They live for Christ within any philosophy and doctrine. They live for Christ reckoning their call and living the life of a true student in ethics, manner and doctrine.

Third, Jesus did not call perfect students and it is impossible for any student to be perfect as learning is a progress occurrence. Jesus, as the Master, is the only perfect and He called His students to grow into perfection as they stay in the school. They may stumble and, of course, the twelve students of Christ acceded into multiple failures in their walk with Him, but they did not quit. Quitters are not part of the school of Christ.

Acknowledgement

This book offers a revision of my teachings in local congregations. It is also the result of my extensive readings and earnest passion to be a true student of Christ. The writing of this book brings to reality my many years of passion to be a true follower of Christ and my longing to see the followers of Christ to be the students/ Disciples of Christ.

In writing this book, I would like to extend my deepest gratitude to my wife Ebise Tuji, my son Soolan Wasihun Senbeta, my two lovely daughters Darmii Wasihun Senbeta and Suudii Wasihun Senbeta, who were very eager to see the completion of this book and patient in not getting enough time while I was writing this book. I also take the initiative to thank my father Rev. Senbeta Gutema and my mother Amane Tolla, who were committed to pray and encourage me towards a successful completion of the book.

It is also a privilege and an honor to acknowledge the contribution of Rev. Bulti Fayissa and Dr. Gutu Olana Wayessa for successfully reading, commenting, critiquing and shaping the completion of this book in the right direction. They deserve much and deserve the best of the many thanks I owe.

Finally, I would like to extend my gratitude to my Master of Theology degree mentors at the Western Theological Seminary in Holland, Michigan. I also thank my MA instructors at the University of Baltimore for boosting my academic writings. I specifically learned a lot from the Western Seminary professors' expositions of the word of God and their academic writings. Their years of contribution made this book a reality. Thank you so much.

Introduction

In writing this book, I came to the understanding that I know little and my knowledge is finite. This book opens a door for critics, writers, teachers, students, and scholars to edify the followers of Christ and deeply root newcomers in Christ, help them understand that they are called to be the students of Christ, no less or greater. While it is a piece of an iceberg, especially for people of Ethiopian origin, this book is the first of its kind to challenge each of us and the global community. This book came into a reality out of the passion I had to be a true student of Christ, and out of the struggle with the life that I have and others have in Christ.

A decade ago, I was attending a church service in Washington, DC and looked into my life and the life of others attending the church and raised a question if I was a student/ a disciple of Christ or a mere follower. I then began teaching on Matthew 4: 18–22 where I was totally dumbfounded of how Jesus called the four students; Peter, Andrew, John and James and made them not anything but the students of Himself who were to live the life of their Master in totality.

Captured by the specific Matthew's chapter (Matthew 4: 18–22), I started to examine what it means to be a student of Christ; what does it mean to be called, and what does it mean to follow Christ. This book explicates and answers all these questions in depth and counters our understanding of where we are in Christ, poses questions to examine our lives and look into the lives of the church comers, new members, and how to help them grow towards true studentship.

The book states that one must be a student and then follow the path of studentship. The book states that one's salvation and becoming the student of Christ are inseparable occurrences in the life of a believer. The book also attests that to be a student of Christ does not require scholarship; it does not necessitate a profound knowledge of something or someone. Instead, it needs the irresistible presence and the coming of the word of God. An instant submission and devotion of the disciples to the call of Christ was simply a divine act operated in God's divine word.

The book has four chapters, each of which explain what it means to be a student from the Old Testament (OT), implications from the New Testament, what features to be a student of Christ comprises, diversity, and if one is called to be a student or a Christian.

The twelve students of Christ are discussed in this book giving a life nourishing word for anyone who commits to read, teach and preach. Backed by the behaviors of each student among the squad of Christ, it offers what our behaviors as believers and students of Christ should look like. It details nominalism, emotionalism, and what to be a music driven but not a student or a disciple is.

Taking examples from diverse Ethiopian Christians, the book also gives analysis of where we failed to build true students of Christ. Giving a concluding remark, the book helps any reader, church pastor or leader to be a student, live a life of the student of Christ and have a paradigm shift in our thinking of what it means to be saved

1

Student in the School of Christ

God is all powerful. He is omnipotent. He does anything by Himself, but nothing is done without Him using His hand made creations as a vehicle. Among His creations, humans are the single most important and unique creatures in His image. Humans are an important and unique source for the operation of God's purpose in this world.

Humans are exceptional for the completion of God's purpose in creation history and God began using humans as the power through which He manages, administers this world from the onset of the creation. God also uses humans to reach out to His creation. He delegates humans to go for Him. He delegates humans to prepare a way to escape punishments as in the preparation of the Noah's ark to redeem His creation. A critical look into Hebrews 11: 7:

> By faith Noah, when warned about things not yet seen, in holy fear built an ark to save his family. By his faith he condemned the world and became heir of the righteousness that is in keeping with faith.

Noah was an important errand of the Lord for the rescual of God's people. As seen from the passage (Hebrews 11:7) Noah built an ark to save the family. This saving did not occur without his call and without his obedience. His call was God's divine choice where he was favored by God as in Genesis 6: 8 "But Noah found favor in the eyes of the LORD." The word "favored" in this passage is χάρη in Greek (accusative case), which means grace.

Grace is a free gift. It is not a human endeavor. This divine grace called Noah into a mission of recusal. The recusal is a delegation. Delegation never precedes a call. Noah's call was divine as one observes from his birth that he was a comforter. One cannot be a comforter because he/she is born to a certain family or a certain group.

Genesis 5: 29 states, "He will comfort us in the labor and painful toil of our hands caused by the ground the Lord has cursed." According to this passage, comforting is of a divine origin. Unless it is of a divine origin in the call of Noah, it is impossible to predict the comforting power or one's comforting ability from the fetus. Accordingly, Noah's comforting ability was prophetic with its source from God. Comforting in the painful toil is especially a divine gift. One deduces from this that Noah was called from his birth for the mission of rescuing. He was called to be an errand person for God.

In general, Noah's recusal mission ejects into our mind and spiritual life that humans are important vehicles for the mission of God. They are agents of salvation. Humans do not have a divine saving power but are messengers of the power that saves. They are ark makers where individuals flee for salvation. But humans cannot be ark makers without the divine call that initiates the mission entrusted to him/her. An ark making does not come before the call; the call moves someone to make the ark.

Making an ark is costly, laborious and time consuming. It is also a mocking for a preacher who says that death is imminent without any substantiating evidence, yet expressing the need to prepare to escape. John Macarthur (2001, p.63) described the situation as 'people passing would point to him, touch their heads' and say, "There is that "fool" Noah." This depicts that the mocking comes from the society which also affirms a separation of Noah from his societal and close friends for the sake of God's call. This separation from the surrounding society and the friends around is costly and painful. Losing the people you know for the sake of God, abandoning your routine daily chores for the divine mission, focusing on a divine task by faith is challenging and at times a tool for mocking. Spencer W. Kimba, (2006, p.140–41) described the mocking as follows:

> As yet there was no evidence of rain and flood. His people mocked and called him a "fool". His preaching fell on deaf ears. His warnings were considered irrational. There was no precedent; never had it been known that a deluge [or flood] could cover the earth. How foolish to build an ark on dry ground with the sun shining and life moving forward as usual!

Another example is the call of Moses. Moses is by far the highest exhibition of divine calling. At a time when a decree was passed by the Egyptian Pharaoh to kill all the new born Jewish boys to contain the population growth of the Jewish people (Exodus 1: 22), a divine recusal hand safely hold the infant Moses hand and let him grow in the Egyptian palace feeding from his mother's breast. One does not need to grow in the palace to be chosen for the divine mission but the case of Moses was an extraordinary miracle accompanied with a divine call.

Growing in the palace, growing as the child of Pharaoh's daughter, seeing no tribulation in life, Moses' chores as a shepherd of sheep in Midian is strongly striking. It strikes because it is strange and uncommon to see a palace boy become a shepherd in a desert Midian, where life is too dangerous due to the harsh climate, lack of resources and a different environment. Moses drank both from the palace luxury life and the Midian desert. In both, the divine calling hand of God was vivid. Without the divine calling, one cannot escape a government decree of manslaughter and for that matter grow up in a palace and taken as the son of the king's daughter. Indeed, it was a divine call and it was a divine preparation for Moses for a mission as a freedom bearer into the Promised Land.

From the Egyptian palace to the Midian desert and back to Egypt as a freedom fighter under the supervision, guidance and help of God was an extraordinary miraculous call. This call cost Moses his palace luxury life and took him to a desert for four decades (Acts 7: 23, Exodus 7:7). It then took him back to Egypt as a bearer of the freedom flag.

Moses objected his call for mission as he considered himself inadequate, fearful, and ineloquent speaker, as in Exodus 4:10. He was not confident that he could accomplish God's mission. In these weaknesses that Moses listed, God was looking a leader, a powerful person tested in a palace, as a shepherd in Midian and in the future wilderness. Moses' weaknesses that Moses himself counted were all not able to hold anything in the presence of a divine power that uses the inadequate for a divine mission. God calls the insignificant, the infants, the stammering, the fishers, and the shepherds for extraordinary divine rescue mission.

Let us look at Exodus 3: 1–8:

> Now Moses was tending the flock of Jethro his father-in-law, the priest of Midian, and he led the flock to the far side of the wilderness and came to Horeb, the mountain of God. ² There the angel of the LORD appeared to him in flames of fire from within a bush. Moses saw that though the bush was on fire it did not burn up. ³ So Moses thought, "I will go over and see this strange sight—why the bush does not burn up." 4 When the LORD saw that he had

gone over to look, God called to him from within the bush, "Moses! Moses!" And Moses said, "Here I am." 5"Do not come any closer," God said. "Take off your sandals, for the place where you are standing is holy ground." 6 Then he said, "I am the God of your father, [a] the God of Abraham, the God of Isaac and the God of Jacob." At this, Moses hid his face, because he was afraid to look at God. 7 The LORD said, "I have indeed seen the misery of my people in Egypt. I have heard them crying out because of their slave drivers, and I am concerned about their suffering. 8 So I have come down to rescue them from the hand of the Egyptians and to bring them up out of that land into a good and spacious land, a land flowing with milk and honey—the home of the Canaanites, Hittites, Amorites, Perizzites, Hivites and Jebusites.

I. Implications for Studentship/Discipleship

Studentship/Discipleship occurs with the introduction of God to the person He chooses. In the case of Moses in the Old Testament, it was God who introduced Himself to Moses in the burning bush (Exod. 3:10–16). This introduction avails that God communicated with Moses and let Moses know that he was chosen to lead the people of Israel out of the Egyptian mastership.

Introduction, choice and call are very important. Moses did not introduce himself to God. It was God who introduced Himself to Moses and called him to a leadership position. Leadership does not happen in the blink of an eye. It passes through training that involves hardship and commitment. Hardships and commitments for Moses began from his birth. He escaped death and was sent to the palace, which he abandoned for the sake of his people under God's guidance. He became a herder in the Midian desert, taking care of his father in law's sheep (Exodus 3: 1). To become a herder from the status of a palace boy is incredibly costly. The cost is that all the luxury lives in the palace were abandoned for the life of a desert, where finding important stuff for life is extremely difficult. These all could not happen without God's choice, God's call, and Moses commitment and obedience, which led to his training.

The call in Moses case was a complete divine program. Moses did not program it. It was not his plan. It was not what he intended. From his birth to the story of the burning bush, to the Midian life and to his standing in front of the Egyptian Pharaoh, his call was absolutely divine. There was no contribution from Moses. All in all, it was God's introduction of Himself and God's divine choice and call. This divine choice, call, and introduction are the same as the introduction, call, and choice of the students/disciples of Christ from around the Galilean Sea, as described in Matthew 4: 18–22.

In both the Old Testament and the New Testament, it was God's divine call that initiated the choice and the call of individuals for His mission. Jesus Christ was the founder and the one who called/calls individuals into studentship/discipleship or the "matheetees" in the New Testament. In Moses' case, although no theologian has depicted Moses as an example of divine studentship, it is asserted from his call, how he abandoned the luxuries of Pharaoh's palace, and how the Lord trained him fits into the New Testament studentship process. Among these processes, the call of an individual and the immediate abandoning of one's belongings and priorities in life in the New Testament assert an exact reflection of Moses' call into the studentship process in the Old Testament.

Also, Moses leadership began as a student in the studentship process but not in the actual classroom but as life experience and communication with God, which led to his leadership career – a proven leader in history. One cannot be a leader without learning, and learning begins as a student from anywhere.

Studentship in the kingdom of God involves a total commitment and obedience even at a time when things do not look promising and guaranteed. Noah was called into that unthinkable building project of the ark in a seemingly unattainable environment, and unconvincing time. But the call, accompanied with complete obedience beyond rationalization and logic, came to be a reality as Noah continued to build the ark. At the very odds of the life situation around him, Noah was obedient. There was no rain; he was in the desert preaching that punishment is coming. People around him were undoubtedly mocking saying, "the fool Noah," as he was busy working on his ark project and as he was preaching the coming of the flood (Macarthur, 2001, p.63). Obedience, and only obedience, defined Noah for 120 years in this career. This obedience was a "gracious obedience," according to Macarthur (p. 67).

"Gracious obedience is a loving and sincere spirit of obedience motivated by God's grace to us. Though often defective, that obedience is nevertheless accepted by God," according to Macarthur (2001, p.67). God's grace is the author of this obedience and, from the beginning; Noah was a man of grace. The grace was not Noah's invention. and grace cannot be individual's invention; it is a gift and Noah was clothed with that grace from his birth that grew in his life and finally made him surrender into a complete obedience leading into a completion of a mega project that easily may hold about 7000 species (p. 65). This mega project was the result of obedience and commitment, both of which are features of a true student of God. These features connect both the calling of the twelve disciples of Jesus in the New Testament and those who were set apart in the Old Testament.

As a conclusion, in both the Old Testament and the New Testament, calling and choices of individuals for God's mission is divine. In both Testaments, calling and choices of God involved commitment, obedience, and separation from the routine daily life for the divine mission. The call and choices also accompanied trainings in a difficult situation for those who were called to bear the tasks and made them complete students of God who, beyond information transfer, grew into the likeness of God.

II. The Old Testament concept of Studentship/discipleship

According to Greg Herrick (2004) the Greek word μαθητής/ studentship or discipleship barely occurs in the Old Testament. Deffenbaugh (2004), quoting K. H. Rengstorf, agrees that in the Old Testament, the concept of discipleship is strikingly absent. Deffenbaugh (2004) notes that men were to be learners of the will of God and estimates that there was no master worthy for the Old Testament people to attach themselves to and thus men were simply servants, not disciples. Hengel (2005, p.16-17) disputes this narrative as he viewed the Elijah-Elisha relationship as a definite master-disciple model, a teacher-pupil relationship as an analogy to Jesus' calling of His disciples. Richard Calenberg (1981, p. 51-63) stresses this notion stating that the Elijah-Elisha model was a master-disciple model with a specific language used in 1 kings 19:21; "to walk." This assertion illustrates that there is a practice of discipleship in the Old Testament. Marcel V. Macelaru (2011, p. 15) concludes that the discipleship in the Old Testament is an imitative in character where the follower copies his/her master.

Macelaru (2011, p. 15) asserts that the Old Testament concept of discipleship is found in the Hebrew word הָלַךְ "haalak"and it's derivate, which expresses one-on-one relationship. This relationship is "walking in the way of others," imitating the life of service and commission. According to Herrick (2004) the concept is elucidated as:

> People committed to following a great leader, emulating his life and passing on his teachings. In these cases, discipleship meant much more than just the transfer of information. Again, it referred to imitating the teacher's life, inculcating his values, and reproducing his teachings. For the Jewish boy over thirteen this meant going to study with

a recognized Torah scholar, imitating his life and faith, and concentrating on mastering the Mosaic Law as well as the traditional interpretations of it.

This explanation depicts the growth of the person to be a follower into the likeness of his/her teacher. Macelaru (2011, p. 15) shares this notion describing the Old Testament studentship/discipleship as imitation, walking in the way of another person worthy of following, which is a typical example of the disciples' call to follow Christ in the New Testament, copying the life of Jesus Christ (Greg Ogden, 2016, p. 82).

In summary, both Noah and Moses disclose how God calls individuals for His mission. Neither Noah nor Moses expected the divine call. The call was entirely a move from God who always calls individuals in unthinkable time and from unthinkable environment for His purposes. The call of Noah to build a mega project; the saving boat and obedience mirror the New Testament discipleship. Also, Moses' obedience and repudiation of his security for the call of God is an exact Old Testament student call and studentship that shows a clear picture of the New Testament call of disciples and the discipleship process.

a. Moses and Joshua

1. A matter of learning

According to Richard Hays (2012, p. 6-8) of Duke University, Moses leadership was not featured by aspiration but a divine call, where God spoke to Moses that he will be sent to Pharaoh to take the Israelites out of Egypt (Exodus 3:10). This call was also accompanied with compassion according to Hays (p. 7), where Moses identified himself with the Israelites in compassion so that God would forgive their sin or else his name be bolted out of the book of life (Exodus

32: 30-32). Moses was also a dynamic listener, whose listening skill shows his dependency on God at all times. Moses did not act without listening to God, and God was Moses guidance book throughout Moses leadership career.

Moses, whose leadership career was built from taking a stand as his Israeli fellow brothers were beaten by Pharaoh Slave masters was by far a gifted leader in the Bible. Despite the luxury lives he was enjoying in the Egyptian palace, he was not willing to accept slavery of the Israelites and decided to take action. He spoke against injustices made against the Israelites and killed an Egyptian, which later led to the departure of Moses to Midian (Exodus 2:11–25). Moses took this action of departing from the palace life as Pharaoh was to criminalize him in retaliation for the killing of the Egyptian. Moses did not compromise his actions; he did not hesitate and was committed to his conviction of taking a stand against injustices. According to Rabbi Evan Moffic (2014):

> Moses is passionate about justice. It awakens him to empathy with his fellow Israelites. It leads him to act to defend them. It leads him to defend the helpless Midianite sisters at the well. It leaves him no choice but to accept God's call to lead the Israelites to freedom. Moses knows who he is. He knows what is important to him. He is not only called by God. He is also called by a vision of a world redeemed.

Moses was also a leader who was committed to passing his leadership career. He was not a dictator, neither was he a leader guided by his own human passion and understanding. He was dependent on God and he was grooming someone to replace him. According to Hayes for Duke University (2012, p. 9) "even the greatest leaders never fully finish the work. They must anticipate not only their own mortality but also the need to raise up other leaders to follow them." Accordingly, in Hayes (2012, p. 9) words:

Moses told the people of Israel, "The Lord your God will raise up for you a prophet like me from among your own people," and he solemnly admonished them to "heed such a prophet" (Deuteronomy 18:15–19). He specifically identified Joshua as his chosen successor and commissioned him to carry forward the task of leading the people into the land, under the Lord's guidance (Deuteronomy 31:1–8). "Joshua son of Nun was full of the spirit of wisdom, because Moses had laid his hands on him; and the Israelites obeyed him, doing as the Lord had commanded Moses" (Deuteronomy 34:9). An important part of the responsibility of wise leadership is to identify and raise up the next generation of leaders to follow, and to "lay hands" on them in blessing to carry forward the unfinished work.

Identifying someone to replace him and committing him to the full control of the Lord in prayer, Moses exhibited how to faithfully fulfill the leadership roles. Moses did not stop in prayers; he also assigned responsibilities and duties of various types to Joshua. Joshua was Moses servant according to the scripture (Exod. 24:13; 33:11; Num. 11:28; Josh. 1:1) quoted in Marcel V. Macelaru (2003, p. 15). As a servant, Joshua's responsibilities were providing for the needs of Moses and acting as a deputy in the absence of Moses (Josh. 17:8; Num. 32:28).

Macelaru (2003, p. 15) explains that Moses' behavior towards Joshua is telling: he commissions Joshua by transferring his authority to Joshua in the sight of the Israelite assembly (27:18–23), he teaches Joshua in various occasions (Deut. 3:21; 31:7–8) and he rebukes Joshua when needed (Num. 11:28–29). All these, one may argue, are characteristics of a master–disciple relationship in the ancient world. Contrary to this, Joshua's leadership was also a completely different leadership style. Moses was more of an intermediary in times of the

Israelites rebellion against God. Moses united with the people and sought God's forgiveness and, if not, preferred his name to be bolted out of the book of life; an extreme commitment to the people he was given by God. Joshua was playing a neutral role amidst the national backsliding of the people of Israel (Josh. 24:15). Although Joshua was not in an imitative personality in his leadership style, it was a rebuke to history to bypass how his leadership was built and shaped under Moses.

Joshua's leadership was connected to a matter of learning from his predecessor. This learning between Moses as the disciple/student maker and Joshua as a disciple/student for future leadership career was not an imitative model but a relational teaching where the teaching sank into the life of Joshua and produced a leader of great reputation in the face of the Jordan river, the down fall of Jericho and the importance of holiness in front of God even when the nation of Israel was to slide back.

b. Elijah- Elisha

2. A matter of renouncing

When God calls people into His kingdom and ministry, there are always things that need to be renounced. The word renounce refers to forsaking or rejecting not only something that is not valuable but also what is precious when a call comes to individuals from the call initiator, the Lord God. As God was the cause of the call and not Elisha, one observes that God demanded the renunciation of the happiness and joys he got from what he owned.

Elisha was farming with twelve yoke of oxen and he had a mega agricultural business. These were his sources of safety, security, happiness, joy and a guarantee of the future. Elisha repudiated everything for the sake of the call. The call was a priority over the prosperities that he had. 1 Kings 19: 19–21 assures this:

So Elijah went from there and found Elisha son of Shaphat. He was plowing with twelve yoke of oxen, and he himself was driving the twelfth pair. Elijah went up to him and threw his cloak around him. Elisha then left his oxen and ran after Elijah. "Let me kiss my father and mother goodbye," he said, "and then I will come with you." "Go back," Elijah replied. "What have I done to you?" So Elisha left him and went back. He took his yoke of oxen and slaughtered them. He burned the plowing equipment to cook the meat and gave it to the people, and they ate. Then he set out to follow Elijah and became his servant.

To sum up, the call from God always demands some sort of giving up (G.T. Coster, 2011). If we are not ready to give up something, then we will not be ready to follow. The matter of following God, the matter of taking a footstep towards the directions of God, is a matter of giving up. It is a matter of renouncing and repudiating the things that we consider valuable.

The call of God is compared to nothing and the call is much more secured than we think as the one who calls us into studentship is trustworthy much more than we imagine. The pairs of oxen, a total of 24 oxen that Elisha was using in his farming industry, and his equipment that were the sources of his livelihood were all renounced at the call of God. They were renounced not because something more valuable is at hand but because the one who provides invaluable stuff and the one who takes Elisha's security and futurity into His own hands is calling.

When God takes your future into His hands, assailing the ship towards where the Lord needs is more important than anything. That was what happened in Elisha's life and the same thing is what God is looking for in our lives as we walk with Him. God wants each of His students, each of His followers who take the steps of studentship/discipleship to repudiate the extra precious stuff in our hands.

3. It was an instant call

The Elisha-Elijah way of Old Testament discipleship was an instant call that moved Elisha to abandon his routine daily farming industry to follow the prophet Elijah. Elisha did not take time to anticipate and count what may be happening in his life. He did not know Elijah very well and did not know what will happen to him in this mission, but he dropped everything valuable for his life and followed Elijah. This following was instant and divine-directed mission. Elijah acted under divine mission in his talk with Elisha and the departure of Elisha was according to the divine direction. The instantaneous call was, however, in God's timetable. 1 Kings 19: 16 affirms this: "Also, anoint Jehu son of Nimshi king over Israel, and anoint Elisha son of Shaphat from Abel Meholah to succeed you as prophet." This instant call mirrors the New Testament calling of the disciples of Christ.

4. It was a matter of Divine Act

A clear observation of Elisha's call depicts that it was a divine act. There was no contribution from Elisha's side. G.T. Coster (2011) explains that Elisha did not expect the divine call. He was in his own agricultural business at the time of the call and had no clue of the divine call coming into his life. Coster (2011) further details that Elisha was sought; he did not seek. God saw him in the rural obscurity and challenged him forth into the national recognition and service. Elisha was called into this distinguished position of the Development of Divine plan (J.Waite, 2010) not because of his career nor because of his background, but because of the God who sought him.

5. A matter of taking irreversible Action

The seriousness of Elisha and his irreversible action towards following God under Elijah's leadership was spectacular. It was spectacular as it demanded the burning of the old equipment. Elisha did not take direction from anyone to change his old equipment, invaluable stuff into ashes. It was the call that propped his heart for God that pushed him to do so. The invaluable equipment that he was using for his farming industry was money and the sources of his livelihood, but Elisha changed them into ashes without any hesitation, considering it as his cost of following God.

What Elisha did echoes what the disciples/students of Jesus did immediately as they were called by Christ, as described in Matthew 4: 18–22. The disciples of Jesus left all their old equipment, a source of their livelihoods and a guarantee of their future for the sake of following Christ. They abandoned their boat, their fishing nets and all that are associated with their fishing industry for the matter of following Jesus Christ.

In summary, the matter of divine call demands the renunciation and repudiation of our old equipment of any kind. The call from God is a matter of living one's own routine chores, abandoning a farming field, quitting a profession, and a matter of burning all old stuff, old habits, old manners, old gods and securities of any kind. This notion asserts that discipleship/studentship is not an easy-believism. It demands complete dependency and assurance on God. Easy-believism is not where the students of Christ nor those who were called to follow God's direction in the Old Testament were called for. All believers are called to follow Christ in deep assurance, copying the life of Jesus and soaked in the purpose of Christ.

6. A matter of complete imitation: Crossing the Jordan river

A key component of studentship/discipleship in the Old Testament is the power of imitation. "To imitate means to follow as a model, to copy or emulate," (Merriam Webster Dictionary, 2019). In this regard, one clearly observes the imitation or the copying principle that was applied in the Elisha-Elijah discipleship scenario. Elisha, following his call to follow Elijah under God's guidance, began to copy the life and ministry of Elijah the prophet. According to 1 Kings 19:16, Elisha was to take over from Elisha in the words of Marcel V. Măcelaru (2011, p. 16). To take over depicts that it was a transfer of ministry – for that matter a transfer of prophetic call from Elijah to Elisha avowing a complete imitation model. The imitation model was clearly observed in the division of the Jordan River at the end of Elijah's ministry and as the onset of Elisha's prophetic ministry. Măcelaru (2011, p. 16) summarizes the Elisha-Elijah imitation model as the:

> Outcome of Elisha's commissioning as prophet, for what he does is identical with what Elijah before him did. All these indicate a successful master–disciple relationship, clearly formalized, having well-defined objectives and leading to successful completion, that is, to the fact that Elisha becomes like Elijah.

7. A matter of joyfulness

Simon Guillebaud (2011, p. 24) quoting Hudson Tylor made the following observation: "Unless there is an element of risk in our exploits for God, there is no need for faith." Guillebaud (p. 24) states that believers faithfully do so many good stuff but never take a single risk. People avoid risks because they believe that they are susceptible to failures and no one likes to fail. Guillebaud (p. 24) writes that those who take risk are successful. Despite the fear of failures and setbacks in business or in faith, those who take risks are successful.

Success creates joy but joy does not come only from success. It also comes from taking risk in repudiating once belongings for God. Elisha was not joyful because he was successful, but he joyfully renounced his prosperities to commit himself for the call of God. He left his farming industry. He slaughtered his oxen, and burned his agricultural equipment joyfully to follow Elijah. In doing so, Elisha by far renounced his security. In renouncing his securities, Elisha risked his life. Out of this risk taking, joyfulness in following the prophet Elijah sprang out.

The price of risk taking in abandoning one's belongings for the highest mission, the mission of God, produces joy of a lifetime and beyond. "The elements of risk taking in our exploits for God," in words of Guillebaud (2011, p. 24) and giving up stuff (G.T.Coster, 2011) are the key in prioritizing the Lord in one's call to be His student for a lifetime.

Studentship in God is a matter of taking heavy risks in life among which abandoning once security is a priority. In abandoning a security of oneself, students of God make God the single incomparable security of a lifetime. The secret of Elisha's joyfulness was hidden in the power of God who took the security of Elisha into His own hands. When the security of Elisha fall ultimately into the hands of God and a full control of God was guaranteed, it created joy in the life of Elisha, who joyfully left his worldly prosperities.

Prosperities are the means of joy for many, but they do not give lasting joy, for lasting joy are anchored in God. The power of joyfulness in God enabled the students/disciples of Jesus to abandon their livelihoods and take the adventure of a lifetime. Guillebaud (2011, p. 24) writes that the "matter of following Jesus is an adventure. It is a journey of unpredictability, full of unexpected detours-sometimes distractions and dangers too- but we have the confidence in the one who is leading the way. He is the Good shepherd."

As a Good shepherd, Jesus is the ultimate guarantee of our security amidst a complete abandonment of our securities prioritizing Him. Elisha's journey was fully guaranteed and that was why the Jordan River was not standing before him. God is faithful in front of the many Jordan Rivers that His students face in life. No Jordan River is more powerful than the God that calls His children into the studentship process of His Kingdom. A safe passage in the Jordan is ahead as the students of God willingly and joyfully sacrifice their securities in prioritizing Christ.

CHAPTER

Studentship in Christ, a New Testament understanding

A Student

What is a student? The Greek word for student is "matheetees"/ μαθητής, and it refers to anyone who is a pupil, learner or adherent. To be a pupil or a learner, one has to have a teacher, which asserts that for "matheetees"to exist there has to be a teacher. The presence of a teacher mirrors the idea that there is a learner or an adherent to the teachings and principles of the teacher. The teacher can be any qualified personnel to teach while the degree of qualification differs.

In the context of the New Testament, the teacher is Jesus Christ and the "matheetai" are those who surrender to Him. According to Doug Greenwood (2007) a "matheetees" is one who surrenders to Jesus and His ways of seeing and doing things. As such, a disciple or a student is one who conforms all aspects of his/her life to the authoritative Lordship of Jesus Christ. This understanding attests that it can be attained through adherence to the teachings of Christ in words and in actions, quantifying the definition that a disciple/student is one who adheres to Jesus Christ. Dietrich Bonhoeffer (1959, p. 48) quantifies this stating that discipleship is adherence to Christ, which affirms that to be a student is to be adherent to Christ. This adherence of learning principles is by no means information transfer in the context of Jesus and His students but imitation, life to life (Ogden, 2016, p. 84).

According to Robert L. (Bob) Deffenbaugh (2004) "a man was known as a "matheetees" or disciple when he bound himself to another in order to acquire his practical and theoretical knowledge." This means of acquiring knowledge is academic. For this academic relationship to exist, there must be a teacher and a student. The presence of a teacher leads to the presence of a student. Deffenbaugh (2004) writes supporting this notion that "there never a disciple without a master or teacher. The teacher was also paid by his disciples." The idea avows that without Jesus a student cannot be, where in fact Jesus paid the price for His students on the cross reversing the notion that a teacher is paid by his disciples. In an actual classroom setting, a teacher is paid by his/her students or the hiring authority, in the context of Christ-student relation, Christ is the one who paid.

Contrary to the understanding that the relationship between the student and the teacher is academic, the relationship between Jesus and His students/disciples has never been academic. Deffenbaugh (2004) asserts that in the New Testament understanding, it is not by any means pedagogical. It is a personal attachment to Christ with lifelong instruction that attests the presence of a relationship where the relationship is "the existence of a personal relationship from the student and a formative power from the Master," in the words of Greg Ogden (2016, p. 64).

According to Leon Morris in Michael J. Wilkins (2004, p. 197), the relationship between Jesus and His disciples was "allegiance to the person of Christ and it is a decisive act." This connotes the notion of following and complete adherence to the person and teachings of Jesus, making them his/her rule of life and conduct. The relationship is unending and a disconnect is unthinkable as Jesus affirmed in Matthew 28: 20 saying "...And surely I am with you always, to the very end of the age," when He was passing the Great Commission. If there is a disconnect that exists, it is only from the student and at no time from the Master. Also, this relationship is not a lecturer-student type as students in this relationship may or may not deduce applications for themselves. It is not that of a prophet merely making a divine pronouncement and leaving the issues of the same. It is a relationship where a teacher pours knowledge into the life of a student with an end goal (Telos) becoming like the Master, realizing the Master's purpose (p. 82). This knowledge according to Ogden (p. 82) was about coping Christ. It was "a life copied" which was the model of the Jewish Rabbis' in the life of their students (p. 82). Taking this model, Jesus was orienting His students into a copy-paste model without a decrease or an increase in the copying method. This "life copying" was in principle a focus on Jesus where disciples were simply in the background, observing who Christ (p. 82) was and what He was doing and taking into their lives. This observation grew in the process of transformation into the likeness of Christ, which is the "telos," the end goal of a disciple/student (p. 81-83).

In general, a student in the school of Christ or a disciple at the onset was in an investigative scenario (Ogden, p. 79). They were examiners and observers as Ogden (p. 63-64, 80) elaborates taking from the Gospel of John, where Jesus said to the 1st disciples to come and see (John 1: 39). This examining/investigative approach grew into the likeness of Christ and in fact into apostleship, which is a sign of delegation. Thus, one observes that the investigative scenario was a divine mission towards the students of Christ who tersely followed to examine. But the Matthew-Mark description is an instant call into discipleship with no investigative approach. It is an abrupt divine call. This does not mean there is a contradiction between the Matthew-Mark writers and John, but one can trace that in both cases there is a divine call and a divine obedience, without which to be a student of Christ never happens. The Lukan discipleship call was a miracle driven as Jesus spoke on the failed Peter-Andrew and John-James fishing team (Luke 5: 10). Jesus' miracle restored the failed business and brought Peter into a repentance and immediate acceptance of the divine call.

One never abandons everything and follows Christ for just investigative purposes only; it is the divine calling power of Christ that is beyond human comprehending ability that propels an instant call to follow Christ. Arguing from my understanding, the investigative drive in the Gospel of John 1: 39 "Come," he replied, "and you will see." was a divine trap into the call; an instant call to be a student of Christ, stressing that there is no collusion between the Matthew-Mark narrative, the Lukan account, and the Johannine description of the calling of the disciples.

The four gospels describe the events as follows:

Matthew-Mark	Abrupt Divine calling	Matthew 4: 18–22, Mark 1: 16–20
Luke	A power driven, Miraculous approach	Luke 5: 1–10
John	An investigative approach	John 1: 29–49

The Call to be a student

You cannot be a student of Christ because you wanted to but because you are called into the School of Christ. This is a drastic contrast from the tradition during Jesus' time where students were choosing their followers (Muller, 1975, p. 488). Allan Carr (2003) asserts that the disciples or students during the time of Jesus were choosing their Rabbis. It was not the Rabbis that were choosing the disciples for themselves. Contrasting this, in Christ's case, the call is directed from the teacher to a student with a demand for response. Any call comes with a demand for response and it can be a missed call if not picked up, but missing a call is also a response. There is a yes or no answer when a call comes from a teacher to a student in the school of Christ. A missed call does not mean the student is not there, but it means the student does not want the call or the student answers during a later time. The best example for this is the call directed to the four disciples and all others around the Galilean sea including the father of John and James; Zebedee in Matthew 4: 18–22. In the same way to the four disciples, a call was directed to Zebedee, but no one sees a response from Zebedee which clears that Zebedee turned down the call.

A yes to the call, on the other hand, is a positive response to the call and a commitment to obey what follows. This understanding asserts that to be a student of Christ is an initiative from the central command, Jesus. D. Muller (p. 488) exemplifies that unlike the tradition during Jesus' time that a follower chose a master; it was Jesus who chose His followers. Jesus also asserted this in His words that it was Him who choose them as in John 15: 16:"You did not choose me, but I chose you and appointed you so that you might go and bear fruit—fruit that will last—and so that whatever you ask in my name the Father will give you."

While this is one way of the call, it can also be from the student to the teacher in which in both cases whether from a teacher to a student or vice versa are a direct connection to the teacher. In both cases the teacher is the call operator and the call initiator towards the student to come into His school. Jesus affirmed this in John 6: 44: "No one can come to me unless the Father who sent me draws them, and I will raise them up on the last day."

This call from Jesus has certain features that accompany it. These features are:

1. It is a divine call

It was neither an invitation nor a call from a human. It was entirely divine driven. It was a God driven program, operated and run by

Him. This divine call is the creative power of God that created the world from nothing. This power makes individuals to say yes to the call. That is how it pulled a tax collector away from his regular chores, and a fisherman from the fishing career to the divine trap of Jesus Christ. The same word has the power to call someone to leave everything and follow Christ instantly. No one has the power to leave everything, abandon whatever he/she has and follow Christ unless the call is divine. Jesus' call was a complete divine power that unconditionally demanded the students to follow Him (Garland, 1996, p. 84) to which each of them said yes. One cannot leave his/her father and his/her boat unless it is divine. The students of Christ choose this path of insecurities that are observed as too reckless, irrational and scandalous (p. 84), but the call to discipleship/studentship looks beyond this world to eternal destiny, which the disciples/students of Christ were assured of that it is best left in the hands of God (p. 85).

As to be a student is a divine call, it is not warranted that this divine call is the same towards individuals in its instant trapping of people into the kingdom of God. While it instantly calls others to begin their walk with Christ with no tangible securities, it may call others later in their lives. The timing is not important here but what is important is the power of the call whether it enacts divine call immediately or later in life as people's response towards the call differs. There are also others that do not at all come to the call. The power of the gospel looks foolishness to some; it lacks logic and reasoning to others. The apostle Paul affirms this in 1 Corinthians 1: 18 "For the message of the cross is foolishness to those who are perishing, but to us who are being saved it is the power of God." This statement by no means rejects the importance of reasoning and logic and never downplays its role in the call to studentship/discipleship or the power of the word. It rather indicates that a divine calling power is beyond our reasoning ability. It is beyond our comprehension and logical explanations.

2. It is personal and Public

"Personal and Public" are terminologies taken from Allen Carr (2003) and they are meant that as personal call discipleship is an acceptance of the call and declaration of Christ as a personal savior and as a public event, it is the confession of faith in a commitment to Christ.

Let us see Matthew 4: 18–22 to discuss discipleship as personal and public:

> As Jesus was walking beside the Sea of Galilee, he saw two brothers, and Simon called Peter and his brother Andrew. They were casting a net into the lake, for they were fishermen "Come, follow me," Jesus said, "and I will send you out to fish for people." At once they left their nets and followed him. Going on from there, he saw two other brothers, James son of Zebedee and his brother John. They were in a boat with their father Zebedee, preparing their nets. Jesus called them, and immediately they left the boat and their father and followed him.

According to Matthew 4: 18–22, the call to be a student/a disciple and in studentship/discipleship came to each of them and was not a group call. One can see that there were people who heard the call but did not accept. For example, Zebedee was right there around the Galilean Sea when the call came to each of them. We also are not in doubt that there were other fishermen and the call was addressed to each of them individually, but only few were drawn to the call and began the journey of following Jesus. Allan Carr (2003) notes this stating that "there were, no doubt, other boats anchored there that day," which means that the others were not drawn to the call. The call was thus guided by individual/ personal decision than a group decision. Asserting this, Paul E. Davies (1956, p.10) states:

> The central requirement of faith is personal and individual. Men actually believe one by one, they are forgiven one by one by one they experience God's grace in justification, reconciliation, adoption. No mass movement involved.

This personal call and personal decision making to follow Christ never stays hidden. What is personal and private matter becomes public. This publicity has moved the disciples/the students of Christ to speak and declare the kingdom of God taking all the risks. Allan Carr (2003) avows that "men are called upon to make a public stand for Jesus. They are called upon to publicly line themselves up with Him, His doctrine and His program." This notion depicts that although our salvation is personal and our call is private, we are to stand in public for Jesus declaring His name. There is no room for obscurity once a person has decided the journey of following and once a person has accepted the call.

As students of Christ, in a changing world and secularized environment, with all its risks, the call into studentship/discipleship bestows the power of breaking obscurity. It also takes individuals that have made personal decisions to the call of Christ from their personal private room to the public without abandoning their connection to their Master. A personal, private call in this regard leads to bringing others into the traps of the nets of Christ. That means the personal call is for the many where the individual works to bring others into the kingdom to be the students of Christ. Staying in the personal connection with Christ, the individual goes on to bring others regardless of the risk, where the others decide individually but form a community of believers-thus community of students/"matheetees." The community here is composed of privately decided individuals for the walk with Christ. This community is a church, where a church stands for the disciples beyond time and space.

A church is a community of believers; it is a community of redeemed souls, called individuals for a lifetime commitment with Christ. Luther in Robert Kolb (2009, p. 154) defined the church as "a holy little flock and community of holy saint under one head, Christ." Kolb (p. 154) notes that these little flock are sinners incorporated into the holy community by the word of God that preserves until the last day. Holiness does not go with nominalism. The holiness of the church comes from Christ and the recreating power of the Holy Spirit. As a community, the church is beyond nominalism with a life called and a life committed to live each day, each time anywhere to live for its Master, Jesus Christ.

According to Got Questions (2015) nominalism "is the possession of a baseless name, title, or description." It refers to the life of a believer with no fruit. Such believers are believers whose lives are taken by shallow-believism or easy-believism. Shallow-believism refers to those whose lives are not deeply rooted in Christ and those who are name bearers but lack the fruit of studentship in Christ. Nominalism is thus a belief that has a relation with nominal church goers. According to Got Questions (2015):

> Nominal Christians are Church-goers or otherwise religious people whose "faith" does not go beyond being identified with a church, Christian group, or denomination. They are Christians in name only; Christ has no bearing in their lives. Nominal Christians may attend church and Christian functions, and they self-identify as "Christians," but it is just a label. They view religion primarily as a social construct, and they do not allow it to require much of them in terms of morality or responsibility. Nominalists take a minimalist approach to their faith.

Nominal believers take the call into discipleship/studentship as shallow and lack "an ongoing encounter with God out of which grows joyful dedication and service," (Louise Kretzschmar, 2013, p.312). Nominals attend church services, recite doctrines and share from the communion tables. They are at the fellowships but lack moral ethics, responsibilities and accountabilities of their actions. They may have profound theological beliefs but lack the commitment of following Christ.

The matter of following Christ is not only a matter of genuine commitment but also a matter of intellectual assent (Kretzschmar, p.320). If it is only driven by intellectual assent, it becomes shallow and proves to be what Dietrich Bonhoeffer (1959, p.50) describes as "Christianity without discipleship." In that case, Kretzschmar (2013, p. 314) writes that it is like trying to drive a car without an engine. Such belief is crucial "in affecting the spiritual health and witness of the Christian Church" (P. 314) for bad. The church is not born on the witnesses of the nominal but on the witnesses of the disciples/students of Christ and must continue to be a disciple formed and run by disciples who have committed themselves to Christ throughout the ages.

3. It is At Christ's Clock

Picture credit: the author

It was a sudden unexpected moment for all the disciples fishing around the Galilean Sea when Christ all of a sudden went to their place and let them abandon everything and follow Him. David E. Garland (1996, p. 69) supports this stating that Jesus' call was abrupt appearance without warning. Garland (84) further states that the students of Christ had no time to even transfer any of the equity they had. It was an abrupt call to follow. Since it was abrupt, the call was sudden and unexpected, involving Jesus as the author of the call and the disciples' sudden but accurate response to the divine call.

None of the twelve students did choose this path; it was the ultimate choice of Christ. It was a call from Christ than neither the orator Peter nor the beloved disciple nor the passive ones. The call from Christ then compelled all of them to leave everything they love and follow Jesus instantly. The call enabled them to abandon all they have, including their parents. That is clearly depicted in Matthew 4: 18–22 where the children of Zebedee left their parents prioritizing Christ. "Leaving" in this context is not a matter of forsaking our parents in our responsibility to take care of them or fulfilling our lives' tasks towards them. It is a matter of prioritizing Jesus if there is anything that puts our walk with Christ under question. What matters is also the time of Christ than ours. This timing differs from individuals to individuals. While others decide to follow Christ immediately upon the call, others decide later in their lives. There is no fixed uniform time when it comes to accepting the call of Christ. But one is accurate and certain that anytime of yes to the call is the time of Christ.

In summary, according to John W. Schoenheit (2015) there was a relational discipleship technique that Jesus applied to have His first disciples. Schoenheit (205) disputes that Jesus told people who barely knew Him to give up their occupations and follow Him. He cultivated a relationship with His future Apostles unlike a sudden abrupt calling that led the disciples to abandon everything and follow Him. In a counter perspective, David E. Garland (1996, p.69-76) argues that it was an abrupt, sudden calling. The word of God has the power to restore the dead into life; it has the power to create things from nothing. This power has the power to call people into the kingdom of God without notice and suddenly. The call of Elisha for prophetic ministry (1 kings 19: 21) and the call of the disciples/

students both in Matthew (Matthew 4: 18–22) and Mark (Mark 1: 16–20) are living examples of abrupt, sudden calling that portray the divine power of the word of God.

According to Schoenheit, etal.(2015) for the Sower Magazine 1st quarter, the Bible does not need to give us an account of the discipleship process of all the Apostles. This notion asserts that despite Jesus' calling where that calling was a sudden abrupt one (Garland1996, p.69-76) or a relational method (Schoenheit, 2015), the call to be a student in the school of Christ did not follow the same pattern, but whatever the nature or the method was, the call was divine and at Christ's clock. Christ's clock displays the absence of a uniform pattern of calling but the presence of a specific time of Christ where specificity refers to any month, day or time in Christ's calling.

4. It is a matter of Falling but not Quitting

Not a matter of not falling but a matter of not quitting as Jesus called His disciples. This was the central principle in Christ's school of studentship- discipleship. Jesus did not call the disciples that don't fall. Jesus Himself predicted the disciples' ultimate failure in the gospel of Matthew 26: 31–32 as follows:

> Then Jesus told them, "This very night you will all fall away on account of me, for it is written: "'I will strike the shepherd, and the sheep of the flock will be scattered.'But after I have risen, I will go ahead of you into Galilee."

At the end, all the students of Christ were succumbed in to humiliating failure. This could have caused the end of their mission in Christ's kingdom. The world is full of obstacles and impediments of life and there is high likely that one falls from his journey of faith. This does not mean one quits although the possibility of quitting the walk entirely falls on the follower as in Judas Iscariot. Jesus did not call not falling students, but he called not quitting students like the eleven disciples/students who even at a very dangerous time of the crucifixion of Christ did not quit. They all fell but they did not quit. According to J. K. Rowling in Adam Hamilton (2018, p. 88) "it is impossible to live without failing as something, unless you live so cautiously that you might as well not have lived at all- in which case, you fail by default." Dale Click (2000, p. 10) affirms that "one does not have to be perfect to be the follower of Christ." And Jesus did not call perfectionists, unfailing individuals but un-quitting.

The underlining truth in the call to be a student of Christ is that if we do not fall, then we are divine but because we are humans there is always the possibility of failure. If we do not fall does not mean failure is a choice but it may result as we are in the spiritual battle ground. Disciples are made for war. There is a flesh fighting over the spirit. In this fight, unlike the cost, we are not at the side of defeat. Jesus affirmed that there are troubles but it is defeated in John 16: 33 "I have told you these things, so that in me you may have peace. In this world you will have trouble. But take heart! I have overcome the world." Also, there is the truth that we are in the world but not of the world. As people in the world and as the world is not ours, the likelihood of falling into its traps are there. Falling then does not mean quitting.

Quitting is the end of a walk, but Christ did not call quitters. This avows that "winners never quit and quitters never win," in the words of Ted Turner in Dian Arismawan (2019). The idea states that we are winners because we are called by the victorious Christ. Jesus called us into a completed battle in victory. It means that we are called to fight standing on victory where the possibility of quitting is less likely or if we quit it is the choice of us as individuals.

According to Idowu Koyenikan (2015) quitters quit in a process without seeing the result but as students in the school of Christ we may fail in the process but do not quit for the result. The result is Christ Himself and there is no other result than Christ. He is the result we are given, resumed walk upon His divine call and will continue in the call worthy of our salvation without giving up. Joyce Meyer (2008, p. 287) writes:

> Never giving up means marching into your future with boldness and confidence, seeing each new day as an opportunity to move forward in all the best God has for you and taking each new challenge as a mountain to be climbed instead of a boulder that will crush you.

This boulder that crushes individual followers of Christ is a stumbling block that may lead into a failure but giving up in this situation is not the principle of discipleship/studentship as Jesus called not falling but not quitting individuals.

According to Tommy South (2004, p. 2) "true disciples do not quit following Jesus just because they fail... The eleven failed, but they still loved Jesus and did not abandon their ministry. They returned to their Source of life and power." In summary, falling is not an alternative as we walk with Christ. It is not a choice. It is not a means of abusing the grace of God. It is not a means of making Christ's grace cheap. It is simply something that we may encounter in our lives not as our choice but as a life process.

5. Involved going to the person's place

Jesus went to the Galilean sea, He went to the tax collecting center, and He went among the sick and found them. None of them did find Jesus but the call to find them was from Jesus alone. When He found them, He went to their situation. He sat along the water bank with them. He watched the taxation process that Matthew (Levi) was doing in Matthew 9: 9-12. He went to watch what they were doing and finally took them to His net. Their net was not big enough for Christ, but Christ's net was too big to have all of them at once. Their net was only for the dying fish, but Christ's net was to restore the dying fish. The fish that they were looking for never makes anyone *un*-hungry anymore but the fisher-Jesus that is hunting them here shall make them full throughout their life time. No fish in Christ's net also dies but any fish in Peter's or Johns or other disciples' net ultimately dies not to live anymore. Garland (1996, p. 69) supports this notion stating that "when the fisherman hooks a fish, it has fatal consequences for the fish; life cannot go as before." This implies contrasting notions in that in one way it fits to Christ's calling where the transforming power of God's rule brings judgment and death to the old yet promises a new creation according to Romans 6: 1–11 as elucidated in Garland (P. 69).

Christ's net kills you only to make you start a different journey of life where he/she called into the studentship lives forever. On the other hand, it opens a question if life comes out of fatality. A secular understanding is that death is the end of life. R.W. Perrett (2013, p. 8) quoting Black Law's dictionary writes that "death is the cessation of life: the ceasing to exist..." but in the doctrine of Christ life only comes out of death. This counters the belief that life ceases to stop with death. Jesus said, "Very truly I tell you, unless a kernel of wheat falls to the ground and dies, it remains only a single seed. But if it dies, it produces many seeds" (John 12: 24).

The notion is where are these fishes or where is the fish found? Fishes are in their places, the water. They cannot be found on the ground. That was the reason why Peter and his companions were around the Galilean Sea. Fishes cannot be found outside of a water bank. This articulates that a net cannot catch fish outside of water. For the net of a fisher man to function and catch a fish, the right place is the water bank. Peter and the other disciples were in the right place with the right instrument. The net in their hands properly functions in the Galilean Sea. That is where a fish or fishes are available. In a similar notion, as fishers of men, the students of Christ must go to the world. The world is the only place where lost sheep are found, and lost sheep are reached.

To have people saved, the students of Christ must break their church boundary and go to the world and seek for the fishes. The tool is in their hand; the word of Christ. The call of the student is to reach in love with the divine word which is the only tool, which is the only net to capture the lost sheep. This understanding also applies to those who are churched but not in the Studentship category of Christ. To be in a church does not mean you are a disciple or a student of Christ. The church is in many ways transformed into the likeness of the world than Christ where it is asserted that many of those who are churched are not the students/disciples of Christ.

The church is transformed into the cultural makeup of the world leaving aside her call to be a student/ a disciple of Christ; the only call way into the kingdom of God. Taking this into account Garland (1996, p. 84) elaborates that the disciples are not those who fill out pews in the church, fill out pledge cards, and often help in the church works but they are those hooked by Jesus and whose entire life and purpose is transformed. As lack of life transformation is clearly observed in the 21stc church, it is paramount important that a U-turn into the studentship- a call into the "matheetees" is vital.

The church from its birth is called to be a student and to be into the studentship process of Christ. Discipleship/studentship or to be a disciple of Christ is not a choice for a believer, it is a call. In his book, the Cost of Discipleship, Dietrich Bonhoeffer (1959, p. 50) asserted in harsh terms but indisputably true that discipleship without Jesus Christ is a way of our own choosing. It may be the ideal way, it may even lead to martyrdom, but it is devoid of all promises. Jesus will certainly reject it. He further elucidated that Christianity without discipleship is a faith without Jesus and it remains abstract and a myth (p.50).

6. No hesitation involved

To hesitate is to be filled with some sort of suspicion about the call of following Jesus. As hesitation is a doubt, it is very difficult to follow

Christ. The disciples did not doubt Christ at this moment of their call. David E. Garland (1996, p. 69) asserts this that the disciples were called without warning and they were unsuspecting. There was no room to suspect who Jesus was. They did not even question why Jesus is calling them. With no question and no doubt, they left everything and followed Christ. How they did this may be a question, but the divinity of Christ can make you drop everything and follow without any doubt.

Christ's divinity is above your doubt and hesitation and in this case the divinity of Christ took away all sorts of hesitation and doubt not to follow. It took away any sort of doubt about the future and enabled them to follow without hesitation. Christ's call makes you not to doubt in following Him and thus the students of Christ dropped everything to heed Jesus' call Garland (1996, p. 69). They did not play any delay tactics in following. They did not list pretexts to avoid the call. They renounced, abandoned and left everything to follow Jesus.

In the gospel of Luke (Luke 9: 57–60) some people played delay tactics to escape the call. They presented diverse cases to avoid the call of Christ and in exhibit of their hesitation of the call. They have prioritized burial of their dead and a cheerful good bye to their family members to which Jesus was in abrupt contrast in His responses to them. Jesus was not against the completion of our family responsibilities but He was against the priority. Elisha in 1 king 19: 19–21 was in sharp contrast to these people in the gospel of Luke 9: 57–60 in that he repudiated all his invaluable stuff prior to his proposal to go home and say goodbye to his parents. As for Elisha nothing was left that keeps him from following. According to J. A. MacDonald (2010) the completeness of his renunciation of the world was expressed in his stand to sacrifice the oxen together with the gear. He has already overcome the entanglements of his life (MacDonald, 2010) guaranteeing sure of his voyages with the prophet Elijah. In the exact the same pattern, the disciples of Jesus repudiated everything and followed Christ that avoided any hesitation. There was no delay tactic that they played and if it exists there was no room as all the valuables that might have entangled the disciples were already renounced. This power of renunciation made their dependency on Christ certain for now and the future guaranteeing their walk with Him and removing the doors of hesitation and doubt.

7. No miracle involved

According to Eric Eve (2002) miracle is defined as "a strikingly surprising event, beyond what is regarded as humanly possible, in which God is believed to act, either directly or through an intermediary." Since the act of God is involved in miracles according to this definition, although all miracles are not from God from the Bible's view, miracle has profound effect on the people. It has the power to change things drastically. Also, miracle changes peoples mind and it changes people's decision. It assists you to believe that something is true. It assists you to take something for granted that you will not fail as you have seen the truth already. It builds up your faith and thus gives you confidence of where you are going even if you do not know where you are heading. It gives you confidence in the person that you follow assuring the guaranteed certainty of your future.

David E. Garland (1996, p.76) describes that "these men have witnessed nothing of Jesus' powers and have no idea what His battle plans might be. They do not take a few days to mull over their decisions, to ask their families' permission, or to seek counsel from a panel of religious experts." This supports the Matthew-Mark description of the disciples' sudden abrupt following of Christ. It also affirms that the students of Christ were dependent on the person of Christ than miracles.

At the absence of any miracle, any miraculous manifestation of power from Jesus, they have unconditionally accepted Christ's call and followed. The only power manifestation they can witness was their complete yes response to the call from Christ. One can also convincingly and undoubtedly trace the disciples/students yes response to Jesus' call a miracle difficult to comprehend and beyond human reasoning. C. R.Gianotti (1999, p. 16) writes: "For some, miracles are the means to validating their faith and that God is really there. Unfortunately, this is tantamount to demanding God to prove Himself to us, otherwise we will not believe." Jesus refuted such demands according to Matthew 12: 38–40:

> He answered, "A wicked and adulterous generation
> asks for a miraculous sign! But none will be given it
> except the sign of the prophet Jonah. For as Jonah
> was three days and three nights in the belly of a huge
> fish, so the Son of Man will be three days and three
> nights in the heart of the earth.

Gianotti (1999, p.16) further attest that "even raising the dead will not bolster or bring about faith in unbelievers. And the same is true for believers." Gianotti (p.16) backs up his argument quoting a Bible passage about the rich man and Lazarus, "If they do not listen to Moses and the Prophets, neither will they be persuaded if someone rises from the dead," Luke 16:31

The faith of the students of Christ never depended/ depends on miracles; it depended/depends on the person who called them. Your call never depends on the miracles that you see but it depends on the person who is calling you. This means, miracles are immaterial when the person who calls you; Jesus Himself is a miracle. Seeing Christ is a miracle above all miracles. Seeing Christ, the miracle will give you confidence that hesitation and doubt has no place. This was what Peter and his fellow companions asserted in their lives according to the Matthew-Mark narrative.

Christ is the ultimate miracle to follow. Any miracle happening after Christ is neither superior nor important than Christ. Christ is the giant miracle that we see in our lives. He is the miracle that calls us to follow Him. It is even tantamount important to downplay the places of miracles as magicians perform lots of miracles beyond the human mind. For example, Shin Lim is a magician with "unstoppable force" in American Got Talent, amassing millions of followers challenging those who watch him from every corner of the world and becoming the champion of the American Got Talent. Nobody knows how Shin Lim plays the cards to control the attention of his audience. One is for sure certain that his magic power never goes above card tricks. The power in his play has also no transformational power on the life of his audience. The magic power that he uses to take the attention of his audiences does not operate in the words of mouth nor from a distance. Even if it operates, it has no power to cleanse people from their sin, and transform the lives of people.

Miracles happen anywhere anytime but none of them happen with words coming out from mouth. Jesus was doing things with divine words coming out of His mouth and sometimes multiplying small things and other times changing the existing things into unthinkable material substances. Other times He was putting dusts on people and it had profound effects drastically transforming the mind of the person receiving the miracles and those watching him.

To wind up, seeing Christ is the ultimate miracle to follow and no other miracle is important to us than Christ. As the single unequal miracle in the believers' life, Jesus also does many miracles that contribute to the growth of our faith, build our confidence in Him and shape our walk with Him. Jesus was performing miracles during His earthly ministry but these miracles should not be the center of our faith.

Jesus preformed miracles to show His divinity, so that people would believe in Him. For example Jesus' first miracle at Cana in John 2: 1–11 has the significance of revealing Jesus as the Messiah and the Divine Son of God (Stephen S. Kim, 2010, p. 117–118). According to Kim (2010, p. 117–118) the word "glory," which is δόξα in Greek in John 2: 1 reveals the person of Christ. This δόξα/ glory, a word also used in John 1: 14, discloses that Jesus came from the Father. This also serves that Jesus manifests God by revealing Himself through the flesh. This revelation of Christ is central in this miracle. This miracle (John 2: 1–11) also states that Jesus is the Creator. By using a mere word which is logos; the word that creates, changed water into wine. This Logos is the same word that is used in John1:3 and Genesis 1:1; it is a "preincarnate word" (P. 198). The same word is applied to Matthew 4: 18–22 where Jesus called the disciples to follow Him. Unless it is the divine word; the logs that can create, no one abandons everything and follows Christ.

In both the miracle of changing water into wine and the call of the disciples, Jesus has the power to give new life and the power to call. The wine from the water in John 2: 1–11 shows that Jesus is the giver of a new life, a life that is found in Christ (Kim, p.119). This wine symbolizes a higher life while the water is a symbol of lower life without Christ as stated by Dodd in Kim (2010, p. 119). At the same time the disciples abandoning of their securities accepting the call of Jesus was a unique new life contrasted to the life they were living. That life was the resultant effect of the Logos.

The other miracle recorded in the gospel of John 4: 43–54 is the healing of the official son from a brink of death. This healing took place at a distance beyond space proximity for Jesus. According to Kim (2010, p. 134) it was a healing from a distance where the physical presence of Christ was not important. Kim (p. 134) quoting Sloan states that the healing "was done by Jesus but in the absence of Jesus." The significance of this miracle is the revelation of Jesus as the Messiah who defeats death and liberates individuals from its cruelty (p. 134). It also elaborates that Jesus even now acts beyond time and space. His word can transform people and brings life to the dead.

Jesus is not bound to the physical presence of Himself to change the life of any one or bring life to the dying people; His word has the same divine serving purpose through which He calls individuals to be His students/disciples. The significance of this miracle (John 4: 43–54) is also in the fact that the official and his son are gentiles whose contact with Jesus ushered the manifestation of Christ's power beyond ethnic lines (Kim, 2010, p. 135).

In summary, while Jesus' ministry was accompanied with miracles, the central message those miracles disclose is the glory of Christ. Whether in physical contact or by a word from a distance, Jesus is the living word, the "preincarnate" (Kim, 2010, p. 198) the Logos that creates, transforms and calls people from the power of the cruelty of death into His kingdom. This divine word is the word beyond time and space to call individuals to be the students/ disciples of Christ for a lifetime. The Logos here is inseparable from Christ. It is the person of Christ, the "preincarnate" (p. 198), that calls individuals to say yes to the call and follow.

8. No fear involved

According to Adam Hamilton (2018, p. 1) fear stems from insecurities, increased sense of uncertainties and not sure of what the future brings. Hamilton (p. 5) also states that both men and women wrestle in insecurities, one of fear's many faces. Hamilton states that both men and women develop fear of health, economic collapse, violent crimes, death and dying (p.1-5). Based on this, it is believed that fear is surging according to Molly Ball in Hamilton (p.2) all over the world making fear a universal (p.7) phenomenon.

Fear despite its universality, despite stemming from insecurities, the disciples of Jesus did not afraid of following Christ. They left all their security apparatus, they left their belongings, and they left all their precious stuff that guaranteed their future but did not fear. Repudiating and cancelling all their securities could have put them in fear but unlike that putting their trust in Christ, they took their footsteps towards the future saying no to look back and get entangled in fear.

According to Steve Carlson (2010, p.2) "the eternal destiny of Jesus' disciples is secure." This security is a guarantee for the walk of a disciple with Christ. Anything that happens to the flesh has no power to determine the end of the soul of a disciple. The disciple's end life is eternally destined and secured in the hands of Christ.

They did not fear to follow whom they did not see before but seeing Christ took away fear from their lives. Anyone who gets a ticket for a journey may have some sort of fear whether the place is far or not. At the same time, anyone who is going somewhere whether he /she knows the place may fear, but in contrast to this we do not observe that among the students of Christ. What we see is bold disciples/students repudiating everything and following Jesus. According to Garland (1996, p. 84) "they left their securities, even their livelihoods, no matter how meager or substantial they were, for something new and unpredictable." This could have put fear, uncertainty and confusion in them, but it did not. Jesus shattered their routine daily life and delivered them from bondages of material concerns (p.84-85) removing the power of fear from them and printing their security into His own hands. As long as Jesus is calling you, your passage is safe. As long as Christ is calling you, there is no room to fear.

Fear is the absence of faith in one's life but it is not always true as the disciples feared Jesus in Mark 4:41 that does not indicate the lack of faith. Here Christ is calling His disciples to Himself and He knows where He is taking them. Since Christ is with them in whom they have put their trust, it is clear that there is no room for fear. As stated fear stems from insecurities about the future but as Christ took the insecurities of the disciples into His own hands, the disciples followed without fear. This does not yet mean fear is completely eradicated from the futurity of the disciples as this is impossible according to Adam Hamilton (2018, p. 13). What is astounding yet is the promise of God in Isaiah 41:10:

> So do not fear, for I am with you;
> do not be dismayed, for I am your God.
> I will strengthen you and help you;
> I will uphold you with my righteous right hand.

An exact similar copy of this promise was given to the disciples where Jesus said in Matthew 28: 20 "...And surely I am with you always, to the very end of the age." This simple looking statement assured the disciples' future as secured but not in the absence of fear. There is fear anytime in the world; there will be fear anywhere in the world. Fear is among any race and every one of us has one and the paradox of our time is that despite living in the wealthiest, healthiest and longest living in generations we are afraid (Hamilton 2018, p. 200). Most of our fears stem from bringing in the future into the present according to James Cochran in Hamilton (2018, p. 200). Despite all the odds of fears, the disciples call and walk with Christ was secured. Those who have chosen the path of studentship in Christ are also secured and the Psalmist has assured us with the unbroken promises in Psalms 23: 4 "Even though I walk through the darkest valley, I will fear no evil, for you are with me; your rod and your staff, they comfort me."

9. A call with no expiration Date

Once called and accepted the call, the call is permanently un-expiring. It leads those who accepted the call into studentship of Christ forever, beyond time and space. As it is not expiring, it is built on the promise of Jesus Christ as Jesus said in John 15:16 & Matthew 28: 20, "I have chosen you," and "I will be with you to the end of the earth." Eric Clevier (2020) in Jesus net blog describes the promises of God as "... freely accessible, as we've seen, but they're also accessible all the time..." and they always will be, until our glorious Savior, Jesus, returns!"

Yes, God's promises have no expiration date! These promises encompass among the many Jesus' divine calling power. This divine calling power is the calling of people into His kingdom. People are always called to be students/"matheetees" for Christ and this call is un-expiring. It stays valid to the end of the age.

The call into the "matheetees" /the studentship is incorruptible.

It is not a man-made call and it stays forever overcoming any threatening challenges from the called person or from the outside. This *un*-expiring divine call remains eternal and according to Greg Laurie (2019) "there is no shelf life on the promises of God. When he makes a promise, when he establishes a covenant, he keeps it." Accordingly, Jesus keeps His call and there is nothing that leads to its expiration. This means that people can leave their faith, people may fall, people may backslide, people may reject their call but the call never expires.

Un-expiring call amidst people abandoning their faith in Christ does not mean Christ's grace is cheap. S. C. Lazar (2019, p. 24) quoting Detrick Bonhoeffer states that "Grace is costly because it compels a man to submit to the yoke of Christ and follow him; it is grace because Jesus says: "My yoke is easy and my burden light," in Matthew 11: 28–30. Lazar (2019, p.24) also states that:

> Grace and discipleship are two sides of the same coin. We are at once both absolutely condemned as sinners, and absolutely justified before God. We must be justified by faith, precisely because we are sinners with no way of justifying ourselves. Justification must be imputed to us as an unconditional gift, precisely because there is no ground for our justification in our behavior.

Discipleship is not an activity. It is the call of a disciple to it. To be the follower of Christ is a divine call and the same divine call justifies through grace. There is no way that the justification of a believer depends on personal activities to please the Lord. It is unconditional and there is nothing attached to it for our salvation as a requirement. The call of a disciple is also unconditional and divine. But the call to be a student/ disciple of Christ is costly. It demands complete repudiation of once belongings to follow. This repudiation of our belongings or separation of our current situation to begin a new journey with Jesus is by far costly and painful for the better. Costly grace is not a matter of activity to please the Lord. It is not a requirement for salvation, it is just a call. Thus, unlike what Forde states in Lazar (2019, p-31-32) as discipleship is an activity to be worked out and should be refuted as one cannot be right with God through work, discipleship is a call.

Salvation is inseparable from being a disciple. The salvation of a person and a call into discipleship are inseparable. There is also no alternative ground to follow God. In conclusion, to be saved and to be a disciple is inseparable and un-expiring. They are automatic occurrences in the life of a disciple with no expiration

CHAPTER

The Composition of Studentship in Christ's School

Diversity

Diversity in the words of Esty et al in Green, Lopez, et al. (2015, p. 1) is defined as acknowledging, understanding, and valuing differences among people with respect to age, class, race, ethnicity, gender, disability, etc. All these diversity features among humans depict that humans from individuals to groups and societies are diverse on the basis of unchanging and changing features.

The unchanging features are features beyond the scope of humans to change, decrease or increase. Such human features are skin colors, age, gender, class, geographical origin, etc. These include the origin of Christ's students from Galilee to Judah. The changing features are those that are acquired from societies or resulted from individual endeavors. These features include religion, academic endeavors, skills, political orientations, etc. In the case of Christ's students these diversity features include their professional carriers varying from fishing to tax collection and to Paul's tent making. Generally, these unchanging and changing diversity features are categorized as a choice and not a choice.

Diversity as a choice is the product of individual's or societies' ladders of successes that expose them to a diversified choice, thus acquired diversity (Daft & Lane, 2008, p. 333). These are choices that people make in their lives to make themselves better. These diversity features vary from professional achievements that people gain through trainings to personal interests.

Diversity as not a choice is an instinctive inborn character. These are something beyond the control of individuals or groups. In the case of the disciples of Christ, to be born in Galilee was not the choice of the eleven disciples of Christ and they could not change it. Judas Iscariot was not born in Judea by his choice and he could not be able to change it. The twelve disciples of Christ were all male and they did not choose to be "male." It was natural and they were not able to change it. In all, diversity whether inborn or acquired is a universal aspect of the human race and a matter of to be in diversity in one way or another is simultaneously a choice and not a choice.

Diversity is not a choice because it is global that no one can leave himself/herself aside from it. It includes every race, every individual and every surface of the globe. It is not confined to differences among racial groups only but exists even among individuals belonging to the same race, language and culture. One can bring in here the diversity features among the students of Christ whose origin was from Galilee.

Peter as a Galilean was a completely different personality contrasting the Andrews, James, John, and Bartimaeus. Peter was different in that he was an orator, uncontrolled in expressing himself and depicted as "the mouthpiece of the disciples" according to H Snape (1971, p. 127). Daft & Lane (2008, p. 333) assert that diversity is differences among people in terms of dimensions. The understanding here is that "people" refers to people occupying the same geographical environment, having the same culture and language. It is also a reference to people of diverse environments, culture and language. Daft and Lane (p. 333) farther assert that diversity includes everyone, not just racial or ethnic minorities. In one of the publications of the Penn State University for College of Agriculture Ingram, P. E. (2017, p.2) states diversity as "all of us in our rich and infinite variety." Based on this notion one can argue that diversity is not a choice meaning it is inborn but at the same time a choice.

Bringing this notion of diversity into students in an actual classroom setting, one concludes that students are diverse by nature and they are not by any means the same. If sameness exists, it is because they are in the same grade level or same classroom or even instructed by the same professor. But in true academic setting standard students are not the same. They differ racially, culturally, linguistically, emotionally, academically, place of origin, economics, and family background. This diversity affirms that "no two humans are the same," as Saxena (2014, p.76) noted. Such diversity traits were deeply imbedded in the life of the twelve students of Christ.

Oneness and uniformity have no place in the school of Christ. This was asserted from His call towards people of diverse backgrounds and personalities. Deffenbaugh (2004) states this as there is great diversity among those who are identified as the disciples of Jesus in the Scriptures. The diversity varies from the betrayer Judas to the inner circles: Peter, James and John (Luke 9:28) according to Deffenbaugh (2004).

Although among the twelve according to R.T. France (1976, p. 53) "only Judas Iscariot was called from Judas," the remaining eleven students were from Galilee but possessed several diversity traits that are irreconcilable. The call from Galilee and Judean itself as a diversity trait has special significance. According to Deffenbaugh (2004):

> The significance of this may be easily overlooked. To be a Jerusalem Jew was a matter of real status. To be a theologically trained Jerusalem Jew was like

being a "Harvard man." To be a Galilean was like coming from somewhere in the Ozarks, to be a real unsophisticated, uncultured "country bumpkin.

This idea asserts that to be a Galilean was to be marginal. Grannis, Laffin, &Schade (1981, p. 16) approve this stating that Galilee is the place of the marginal. One cannot be marginal because he/she belongs to a certain geographic setting but because of what the place features. Roland Dienes (2014, p. 18) explains that to be a Galilean would have been characterized as having a politically suspect background, a lack of education, the temperament of a farmer, and a deficiency in orthodoxy. This stems from the supposed absence of the Pharisees, or Pharisaic influence in Galilee which serves as an explanation for the "lack of education" in the Words of Dienes (p. 18). The disciples' lack of education is also depicted in the book of Acts 4: 13 as "when they saw the courage of Peter and John and realized that they were unschooled, ordinary men, they were astonished and they took note that these men had been with Jesus."

To be unschooled means they lacked formal training. This assertion is supported but it does not mean they were foolish (Deffenbaugh 2004). Deffenbaugh (2004) writes that:

Professionally and personality traits of each students of Christ differ drastically. Their economic upbringing also differs attesting the notion that diversity is central in Christ's call of His disciples. This notion goes into their family backgrounds. This can be avowed from the call of Zebedee's Children added to Peter and Andrew who were professional fishermen as in Matthew 4: 18-22 to the Tax collector Matthew in Matthew 9.

As a tax collector, Matthew or Levi was the employee of the Roman government with some educational background related to tax collection or money collection. Economically, as observed from Matthew 4: 18-22 there is disparity among the four Andrew, Peter and the two sons of Zebedee; John and James.

Compelling evidence is that the sons of Zebedee had a boat not a net (Garland, 1996, p. 84) which worth a lot of money but Peter and Andrew had only a net. Having a net for fishing and having a boat for fishing depict the status among the two groups; the Andrew-Peter and the John- James. The Lukan description of the economic status of the disciples counters the Matthew description in that in Luke Peter had a boat (Luke 5: 1-10).

People have never been the same and sameness is unattainable. The world remains diverse in all aspects of diversity elements whether primary or secondary elements. Jesus' disciples were diverse in many ways although they were called from the same place with the possibility of possessing the same language. Dialect in language itself has marked one of the diversity features. For example, Peter's dialect was different from the other Jewish inhabiting in Jerusalem due to which he was caught the night Christ was crucified. This dialectical diversity "reflects the prejudice of a city-dweller against some-one from rural Galilee," according to Deines (2014, p.1). They were diverse in Character in many ways. They were made of the accountant Judas, a man who chose to steal money and at the same time committed to saving money to the doubtful Thomas. In all, they had feckless Characters from recklessly abandoning their master the night he was crucified to complete denial in his Lordship. They were people engaging in nepotism and materialism.

According to John MacArthur (2002, p. 30) the entire synoptic gospels and the book of Acts described the disciples into three groups. The three groups have always been described in order with Peter at the top. Each group has a leader and in all the synoptic gospels and the book of Acts the leaders are the same (P. 30). John P. Meier (1997, p. 647) writes supporting this that the disciples were divided into three groups with the same basic order. MacArthur (p.30) puts the groups as follows:

Group	Matthew 10: 2–4	Mark 3: 16	Luke 6: 14–16	16 Acts 1: 13
Group-1	**Peter**	**Peter**	**Peter**	**Peter**
	Andrews	James	Andrews	James
	James	John	James	John
	John	Andrews	John	Andrews
Group-2	**Philip**	**Philip**	**Philip**	**Philip**
	Bartholomew	Bartholomew	Bartholomew	Thomas
	Thomas	Matthew	Matthew	Bartholomew
	Matthew	Thomas	Thomas	Bartholomew
Group-3	**James (son of Alphaeus)**	**James (son of Alphaeus**	**James (son of Alphaeus**	**James (son of Alphaeus**
	Lebbaeus (surn. Thaddeus	Thaddeus	Simon	Simon
	Simon	Simon	Judas (son of James)	Judas (son of James)
	Judas Iscariot	Judas Iscariot	Judas Iscariot	Judas Iscariot

While the grouping is so interesting, it is unwarranted to divide the disciples into groups where some are considered as too close to Christ and the others are not. MacArthur (2002, p. 31) states that this grouping is based on their proximity to Christ where the 1st groups headed by Peter were considered as the "Inner Circles."

The "Inner Circles" were meant to have access to details of information including some higher opportunities for growth which is highly disputed as Jesus divinely called all of them to Himself and there were no exception among the twelve. MacArthur (p. 32) basis his findings of "Inner Circle" on the fact that the groups considered to be the "Inner Circle" were with Christ at key times. These key times are undisclosed in the MacArthur's account. Among the "Inner Circles" Peter, James and John with the exclusion of Andrews were even too close to Christ other than the others and they were present during the Transfiguration of Christ and in the Garden of Gethsemane (Matthew 17: 1; Mark5: 37; 13: 3; 14:33) according to

MacArthur (p. 31). Their presence during these key events made them the "inner circle" group.

But does the presence of the "Inner Circles" in the key events with Christ designate them as the "Inner Circle?" As all are divinely called and as there is no exceptional attachment to Christ among the twelve or even among those of us who are the students of Christ, it is highly debated that the "Inner Circle" understanding is valid. We all are the disciples of Christ and that has nothing to do with unique attachment, it is a call based on Christ Himself who has no exceptional favor on some and not on the others. Jesus' favor is on all of us equally and without exception. If there are differences, they are only based on areas of concentration on the mission entrusted to us. This concentration is in the specific work given to each of us. Depending on the specific works given to the "Inner Circles," the name is valid. What I do, others in the church do not do. What others do in the church, I do not. We all are different and do different specific activities. These activities make us' "Inner Circle" but have no contribution to our salvation, the grace of God and the call.

The Two Brothers; Peter and Andrews

1. Peter

Peter was the brother of Andrew and was a Galilean by birth. He was the son of Johan according to Matthew 16:17. The gospel of John (John 1:42; 21:15–17 describes Peter as the son of John. A debate may arise why the discrepancy in the name here? It can be concluded that it was a literary discrepancy than something of a theological importance. In Galilee, Peter was born in the specific place called Bethsaida and had a house in Capernaum (Dale Click 2000, p.9). He was also married according to Luke 4: 38–39, where Jesus healed Peter's mother in law. Peter could not have a mother in law without a wife.

Professionally, Peter was a fisherman who was called by Christ while on his career. He had a fishing business around the Galilean Sea possibly run with his brother Andrew according to Matthew 4: 18–22. They were using a net for fishing. Luke, on the other hand, in Luke 5: 3 states that Peter had a fishing boat. Unlike Matthew, taking the Luke's account one traces that Peter and Andrew had a relatively well positioned livelihood that puts them in a better economic position. Having a boat for fishing and a net to run a fishing business elaborates that the fishing industry is run by a better economic footing.

Call

To be the disciple of Christ was not Peter's choice. It was outside of his life plan. There was no contribution from Peter. It was not Peter's initiative to be a student of Christ. According to Bradford B. Baline Jr. (2007, p. 35) Peter did not come to Jesus of his own initiative but "brought." The word "brought" states that he came to Christ through somebody else. The "somebody else" refers to Andrew as he brought Peter to Christ. Beyond the "bringing" what Blaine Jr (p.35) writes is that Peter did not come to Jesus by his own initiative. This explains the truth that Peter was called; he became the student of Christ by the divine call of Christ. This affirms that no one becomes the follower of Christ by his/her own initiative. Whether we are brought to Christ by people like Andrew or any other or by our own willingness, our becoming the students/ followers of Christ is a complete divine program.

Peter had two separate names. His parents named him Simon but as he became the disciple Jesus gave him another name; Peter. Throughout the synoptic gospels and John, Peter was named as Simon Peter or Peter both of which have special significance separately as Peter or Simon or together as Simon-Peter(MacArthur 2003, p.33-36). According to MacArthur (p. 33-34) the two differing names of Peter have special significance. Both names will be dealt later.

Description of his Character

The Rebuke: Peter had a complete feckless character in his call as a student. First, he was the disciple against Jesus' divine plan of imminent suffering. Jesus clearly taught His disciples that He will be suffering in the hands of the Jews, killed and raised from the dead. This was a "shocking inversion," contrary to the Jewish taught that a military messiah who could free the Israelites (Robin Whitaker 2013, p. 670). As Jesus was predicting His ultimate unwavering divine plan, Peter was at odds to it. He did not want the suffering, death and resurrection of Christ. Jesus stated His suffering and death in Matthew 16: 21:

> From that time on Jesus began to explain to his disciples that he must go to Jerusalem and suffer many things at the hands of the elders, the chief priests and the teachers of the law, and that he must be killed and on the third day be raised to life.

Following this, Peter began to rebuke Jesus of His divine Plan. It is read as follows in Matthew 16: 22: "Peter took him aside and began to rebuke him. "Never, Lord!" he said. "This shall never happen to you!"

Peter's mind was occupied by earthly things, expecting Jesus to triumph in the world as a king who liberates the Jewish people. It was an earthly mindset against the Lord's divine plan. In fact, it is the fight between two kingdoms where Peter represents the earthly while the Lord was of the divine. This notion is supported from how Jesus rebuked Peter as "Satan," ἐπετίμησεν. The same Greek word was applied by Jesus when He rebuked demons (Mark 1:25; 3:12; 4:39; 8:30, 33; 9:25). The rebuke was a command to silence the demons and it clearly depicts a power conflict where Jesus overpowered them. The same way Jesus rebuked a power working through Peter.

In rebuking Peter, according to Whitaker (2013, p. 673) Jesus was behaving in a manner befitting a teacher who is correcting a disciple. The correction was because the student Peter was wrong and wrong in seeking what was not in Jesus or what was against Jesus' divine program from the beginning. The rebuke had double purposes as Jesus' words are simultaneously a rebuke and a recall to adopt the correct posture of a true disciple—one who follows and who thinks according to the divine way and not the human way (Mark 8:33). Whitaker quoting (2013, p. 763) Joel Marcus suggests that Jesus' rebuke of Peter "carries the sense of "resume the path of following that he has momentarily forgotten."

Second, according to Whitaker (2013, P. 763) Peter exhibited failure in his rebuke of Jesus, for to rebuke is not the role of a disciple. This means besides an earthly occupied mind set, Peter's rebuke was not of a chain of command. He was a student and a student's role is to take instructions from his/her Master and not in a position to rebuke a Master. In this case Whitaker (p. 763) describes that Peter was inappropriate and Jesus rebuked him saying "go, go away." Whitaker (2013, p. 763) writes that "go, go away," does not mean "leave entirely," but it means "go and get back behind me." This means, be in your right place. You missed your place now; you are in the wrong place. You were called to follow, you were called to be a student but you are taking the Master's position.

Physical Fight: He was a disciple who believed in a physical fight and struck the ear of the high priest's servant (Malchus) in John 18: 10–12 to prevent the arrest of Christ. Attempting to prevent the arrest of Christ in Peter's move was a failure from the start as Jesus was predicting His arrest and ultimate failure in the hands of the Jewish from the beginning. At the same time, striking someone with a sword is an act of violence and Jesus was against any violence in His service and He was shaping the ministry of His future apostles towards that.

Peter was engaging in violence as he used a sword to counter evil. Evil was not and will not be defeated by violence and Jesus rebuked

Peter and astoundingly healed Malchus' ear according to Luke 22: 50–52. What was astounding here was that Jesus was revenging violence in compassion and he resisted it and resisted it to the full displaying a spectacular mercy by immediately healing the high priest's servant, Malchus' ear. Added to healing, Jesus spoke to Peter fiercely and said put back your sword. One then asks why Peter was carrying a sword. Did Jesus allow and did not allow the use of weapons and why was it? Although my knowledge on this is too limited, it is unwarranted that Jesus was at times promoting violence and at times not prompting.

There are people who argue that Jesus was promoting violence as a self-defense (Moyer Hubbard, 2014). This group also says that Jesus urged Peter to put back his sword because it was too late as they were outnumbered at the time of Jesus' final capture (Hubbard, 2014). This statement was driven from Peter's use of a sword against Malchus (Luke 22: 50-52) and Jesus words on Luke 22: 36 "… and if you don't have a sword, sell your cloak and buy one." Hubbard (2014) counters those who argue that Jesus was promoting violence on the basis of the notion that Jesus was not as it was impossible to resist the Roman government by two swords. Jesus countered this argument in Matthew 26: 55 as follows. "Am I leading a rebellion that you have come out with swords and clubs to capture me? Every day I sat in the temple courts teaching, and you did not arrest me." Jesus also rebuked Peter in stern contrast from violence in His compassion towards Malchus and in His statements in Luke 22: 51 "No more of this!" and Matthew 26: 52 "Put away your sword!"

In summary, Hubbard (2014) writes that "Jesus seems to be correcting a misunderstanding of that earlier statement by someone who thought Jesus was actually suggesting that violent resistance was appropriate." Hubbard (2014) also gives the following remarks in countering those who say Jesus was outnumbered:

> …in rebuking Peter and commanding him to put
> down his sword, Jesus was actually saying, "We are

outnumbered at the moment; the time is not right for violent resistance." As Jesus' rationale makes very clear, this is not a "the time is not right" kind of prohibition; it is a "the time is never right" kind of prohibition.

Naming; the double standard behavior: Peter was always at the head of the twelve. He was a leader and a spokesperson (MacArthur 2003, p. 29). The idea of spokesperson is taken from the notion that Peter was always at the forefront speaking. He was also representing them in speaking after the resurrection besides that he came up with a suggestion about the disciple who replaced Judas Iscariot. The suggestion was accepted and Matthias replaced Judas Iscariot depicting Peter as a true leader.

Peter was not his original name. It was not a name given by his parents. His parents named him Simon. The name Simon has special significance in the life of Peter. Simon means vacillating, undependable (MacArthur 2003, p.33). Given Peter's character it is warranted to say that Peter was not dependable as he was giving promises and at times failed to keep them (p. 33). Simon was a disciple of broken promises. Simon was a name typifying an old life which was impetuous, impulsive and overeager (p. 34). It was a name reflecting his natural life; the best example of unregenerate life-a life that was not born again. This was at times displayed in his characters, actions, attitudes and words (p.35).

Simon is the Greek form of the Hebrew name 'Simeon', which is the name of one of the fathers of the twelve tribes of Israel. The name comes from the root word [m;v'*shama'* according to Gen 29:33, which means 'he heard'. Leah said that God had heard her prayer as she gave birth to him, and she named him 'Simeon'.

According to MacArthur (2003, p. 35) Simon of course was his given name and he was referred to by this name in secular contexts. MacArthur (p. 35) bases his findings on specific examples from the scripture as follows: Simon's house (Mark 1: 29), Simon's wife mother (Mark 1: 30) Luke 4: 38), and Simon's boat (Luke 5: 3). Then, MacArthur (p. 35) states that this name has nothing to do with Peter's spirituality or Character. It was a name given to him by which he was identified. But given the meaning of the name "Simon" and the characters that Simon- peter was exhibiting after coming to Christ, it is warranted that the name "Simon" was a clear depiction of unregenerate life or a life that was secular; worldly outside of Simon's call to be the true student of Christ.

Jesus was calling him "Simon" after He even nick-named him Peter showing that the life of Peter was still natural at a time when he was believed to be Peter. According to MacArthur (p. 36) every time, Jesus was calling him "Simon" after he was given the name "Peter," it was a sign of rebuke or admonishment. Simon is thus an example of a person not born again. Such people are people still among the students of Christ and their rebirth takes a process to reach a level of a truly converted believer.

MacArthur (2003, p. 36) states that Jesus called him Simon-Peter fifteen times. According to MacArthur (p. 36), this was an example of two lives. Peter was living a life of double standard even when he was walking with Jesus and Jesus was calling him, "Simon-Peter" when he was to be called Peter. Unlike the name that Jesus gave Peter, the life of Peter was mostly not dependable and exhibiting a natural life style, a life that was not bearing fruits of acceptable standard. He was walking a life that was not pleasing to the Lord or he was leading a life of a baby when he was to be matured enough to be an adult.

Simon is a typical example of a natural life. It is a name that features spiritual infancy when someone is to be a teacher. This life is a life of an abnormal believer whose spiritual health did not follow a normal growth process in Christ. It is undependable which means Simon. Many are Simons when they are supposed to be Peter. Many are Simon-Peter when they are called to be Peter. They possess a life of double standard. They are students of light but still playing in a dark world.

Unlike Simon, Peter is a different name. It means Rock. It was given by Jesus to show that the life of Peter needs to be a Rock-unmovable, dependable. Peter's characters are very dramatic if one looks into the scripture carefully. He is at times a disciple who left everything and followed Jesus (Matthew 4; 18–22). He was also a unique example that possesses a repentant life (Luke 5). He was also sober and sincere, who was too humble to regret for his failures and repent. Peter was also a person who was willing to give his life at a very dangerous place. He was a person who gave his life to come out of a boat to be like Jesus. None of the twelve disciples had that life. He was also the only disciple standing in the courtyard of the high priest house. He did not completely abandon Jesus at a very dangerous time and he was seen by Christ from a close distance.

Peter's life style is generally depicted as:

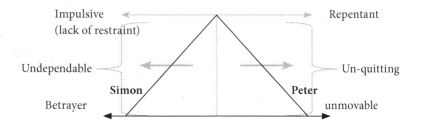

A. Impulsive (Lack of Restraint Behavior): Peter's impulsive behavior is exhibited in his rush to promise and failure to ultimately not be able to keep them. In fact, according to John MacArthur (2003, p. 54) Peter was always "absolute," that he will be doing something. For example, Peter was absolute that he was not going to deny Jesus (Matthew 26: 33). He was absolute that Jesus would not wash his feet (John 13: 8) but in both cases he failed. He was proved wrong. One can argue that Peter's impulsive behavior warrants how emotion driven he was. His violent behavior was also one aspect of his characters. Peter was too quick to take his sword and struck the high priest's son (John 18: 10). He was not restraint but Jesus not only rebuked him but deleted the power of violence in Peter's sight by immediately healing the ears of the high priest's son.

B. Firm-Unmovable: The name Peter was given to Simon when Jesus asked about Himself. In this place, Simon among the twelve answered, "You are the Messiah, the Son of the living God," Matthew 16: 16. In response to this accurate answer, Jesus tapped Simon with a different name; a name completely different from Simon in meaning and depiction of identity. Jesus' response was as follows:

> And I tell you that you are Peter, and on this rock
> I will build my church, and the gates of Hades will
> not overcome it. Matthew 16: 18.

Contribution: Peter contributed a lot in the ministry but a living witness to his contribution among the many is his writings. Peter contributed to the writings of two New Testament letters. Both letters carry his name as a patent right to his authorship. In his fist letter he addressed that believers be strong in faith amidst persecution. Peter stated that believers be strong in faith for two reasons; as a witness for their Christian faith and because of their future hope (1 Peter 1: 1–12) which Kelly observes (Kelly 2007, p. 4) . According to Kelly (p. 4) "those who suffered persecution for righteousness would be vindicated, Christ being the ultimate example," (1Peter 3: 8). Kelly writes (p. 4) that "in these words one detects the strength and maturity of a man who understood his role as a shepherd and elder to the younger leaders of the Christian movement in the Asian minor."

In his second letter Peter writes that believers stand for the truth, oppose false teachings which he addressed echoing the notion that he was the eye witness of Jesus' ministry defending the apostolic teachings against heresy (2 Peter 1: 16–21 & 2: 15–19). According to Dick Lucas & Christopher Green (1995, p. 10) Peter articulated a warning sign that the church would be facing as a pilgrim in this world. Peter lays down the conditions for survival to guard against errors that may lead them to fall from their secured position. It means that Peter values stability (2Peter 1: 12) and expounds in terms of steady growth in favor of God and in the knowledge of Christ (2 Peter 3: 18).

In talking about the truth in the 2nd letter, Peter calls believers to stand for the truth and even if it would cost one's life to which he abandons his life soon as a model. As a writer, Peter produced two New Testament letters, where he encouraged believers to stand firm in faith regardless of difficulties. Also, he propped believers to stick to the truth even if it is pricey. In fact, the truth here Peter is calling believers to stick to it is, Jesus Himself.

Conclusion: Peter's life was featured by failures, backsliding and generally a double standard to its best. He was also a student of accurate vision, unwavering love, sincere and regretful with the coming back heart. He was swimming in two realms while walking with Christ. He was serving both his Master and his flesh driven behaviors ranging from failed promises to standing against Jesus' divine plan by rebuking Jesus and countering in violence those who were to arrest Christ. Beyond these behaviors, Peter was a committed disciple who was determined to take every risk for Christ. He was the one who walked with Christ and took his sword to defend Christ although that defense was unwarranted. Peter was the one who walked with Christ to the courtyard at the very dangerous time. This was where he betrayed his Master but seen from a distant and soberly wept as a sign of true repentance. He regretted not for bad to take his life like Judas Iscariot but as a sign of a repentant soul.

After the resurrection of Jesus, according to Click (2000, p. 11) Peter was the 1st disciple to enter the tomb where Jesus was buried as a sign of dying and resurrecting with Christ. Click (p. 11) also states that Peter was the student who suggested another apostle to replace Judas Iscariot. He was a leader to come up with a suggestion and his suggestion was accepted. Click (p. 11) writes that the first Christian sermon was preached by Peter and thus proved to be the right spokesperson representing the disciples. Peter was also a student who was moved by the power of the Holy Spirit in healing the lame in Acts 3: 1–11 in a direct copy of his Master who healed a lame person in John 5: 1-14. In both incidents, Jesus and Peter exercised divine power where Peter exercised as a called student but Jesus as God. For Peter, it was a copy-paste type of the life of Christ.

Peter was also the first to travel to Samaria and preached being a true witness to the Great Commission breaking cultural and linguistic barriers. Peter proved that Christ was for every race, language, culture and religious entity. Peter was also someone intolerant to lies, "duplicity" of Ananias and Sapphira in Acts 5: 1–11 according to Click (p. 11).

Peter was also a disciple who went to Rome in about AD 61; three decades after the resurrection and willingly (Click 2000, p. 11) and by faith gave his life for Christ. However his life was soaked in double standards at the beginning, Peter proved to be the ROCK for Christ in giving his entire life, not leaving any island of his life for the Master. Despite his mistakes, failures, and too many stumbles, without quitting Peter committed his life for Christ and " practiced what he believed," according to Click (p. 12). He was not taken away by his failures but overpowered all his wrongs by the grace of Christ and concluded his life of commitment as a hero of faith in Rome.

2. Andrew

Brief History and Call

He was one of the four disciples who were called while fishing around the Galilean Sea. He was also the younger brother of Peter

(MacArthur 2003, p. 62). Theologians also believe that he was the one who brought Peter to Christ making him the 1ˢᵗ soul winner for Christ among the squads of Christ. Bobby Kelly (2007, p.1) writes that "Andrew immediately brought Peter to Jesus." Affirming this, Dale Click (2000, p. 15) writes that Andrew was the introducer whose call began by bringing Peter to Christ. This notion is disputed according to Matthew 4: 18-22. According to this text, Andrew was called along with the other three disciples; Peter, James and John and the calling was an abrupt sudden calling that led Andrew to abandon his fishing industry and follow Jesus as a student.

Both Andrew and Peter were the sons of Johan (p. 16) and were grown in Capernaum where they were sharing a house (Mark 1: 29). They were born in Bethsaida but relocated to Capernaum (MacArthur 2003, p.61-62).

MacArthur states that Andrew was a fisherman by trade (2003, p. 16). He was a professional fisherman whose business was run by him and his brother Peter. As repeatedly stated, the two brothers have a fishing business around the Galilean Sea. They were working in partnership according to Click (2000, p. 16). MacArthur (2003, p. 62) also approves this stating that both Peter and Andrew "operated a fishing business together."

Features of Andrew: Andrew is featured by the following in the scripture. His features are completion of simple acts which Dale Click (2000, p. 17) observes:

Hunting Individuals for Christ:
He is the one who introduces someone to Christ; a member of his family, Peter who later became a leader in the teams of Christ. Bringing people to Christ is a commission given to the students of Christ and just from the onset Andrew resumed his call of bringing souls to Christ. He has already known the importance of Christ in the life of people. He also has already known the assignment of a student of Christ which is winning souls-winning souls for the

kingdom of God. In doing so, according to Click (2000, p. 16) "he was bold in faith who unashamedly believed in Jesus as the one who saves." Andrew had the right heart for effective ministry and he gave Jesus to the person he most loved; his older brother Peter. For Andrew, love is driven by giving and if Andrew is asked what to give, his simple answer is Jesus.

Jesus as a reference book:
Andrew was a student who takes people with questions to Christ. There are questions that we answer; there are questions that we direct to those who are above us. There are questions for which we look for references. Andrew knew for sure that Jesus was a reference book for those with questions. Taking Jesus as his reference book, Andrew directed the Greeks to Jesus in John 12:26. Andrew knew that Jesus had the answers. Andrew also knew that humans may or may not have the right answers, solutions to some questions of life. Philip, one among the twelve was hesitant here. Philip was not able to answer the question and run to Andrew for help. Andrew had a reference book where answers are available and he took the Greeks to Jesus who listens to those with questions of life.

Faith in the one who multiplies the insignificant:
Andrew was also a student who takes any small thing, something that looks insignificant to Jesus. Andrew knows that Jesus had the power to multiply any small thing in our hands. He thus referred to Jesus the "five loaves of bread and the two fish," in John 6: 9. Andrew believed in the divine power of Jesus Christ that makes miracles. He believed that Jesus had the power to multiply the insignificant into a huge banquet table millions are served from. Jesus has the power to multiply our small things into a huge food basket for the hungry. The students of Christ for sure know that Jesus is the only one that fills the heart of the hungry people in this world- Jesus the bread of life.

Recognizes resources in the hands of others:
Andrew had the capability of seeing important stuff in the hands of his companions. He was the one who saw the five loaves of bread and the two fishes for huge banquets in the hand of a little boy standing (John 6: 9). When Philip was too pessimistic, Andrew has already known the small resources that could be multiplied to feed the thousands that were gathered around Jesus.

There is no small in the sight of Andrew as long as Jesus is present. Andrew sees beyond circumstances and sees resources everywhere and even among the thought "insignificants." None had seen the boy with the loaves of bread and the two fishes. Andrew was quick to realize that there is a small amount in the hands of a boy among the crowd. The students of Christ are those who see the insignificant, meager looking resources and believe Christ over them that they are enough for the millions, the thousands and the hundreds.

Boldness:
According to MacArthur (2003, p. 64) the name Andrew means "manly" a description that fits his career as his fishing demanded physical strength. It is a Greek name in the form of "Andreas," which means 'manly'. MacArthur (p. 64) further writes that his name depicts his boldness, devoutness and was driven by a hearty passion for truth. According to MacArthur (p. 64) this is inferred from his devoutness to join the teams of John the Baptist, a team cut off from the comfort city life to the wilderness. As a student seeking the truth, Andrew took a bold step to be in the wilderness. Truth cannot be found in our comfort lands, it is found in unlikely places. Truth is found in an unlikely person; the son of a carpenter. Andrew sought that truth and he found it.

Sees Pastors in unlikely places:
Andrew was a student whose spiritual eyes were wide open to see who and what individuals have to contribute for the expansion of the kingdom of God (John 6:9). At a place where no one expected and no

one was able to see; Andrew was able to recognize a young boy who had resources and who was able to feed the 5000 people congregated around Christ. Andrew saw a boy who was too microscopic to the many eyes that served as a pastor. The little boy was made a pastor only because he was seen by Andrew. Andrew did not only see him but the resources in the hands of the little boy. With the insignificant, insufficient looking resources, the boy fed the thousands. What was astounding about Andrew was that he was able to see resources and someone who was to commit himself for Christ. Andrew's big spiritual eyes were focused on Christ in linking the little insignificant resources and the little boy to Jesus. Andrew was confident in Christ that Jesus uses the small boy for his glory.

Conclusion: Andrew among the twelve students of Christ had a typically unique ministry gift of bringing individuals to Christ. He was always focusing on individuals. Andrew had the capacity to influence others for Christ. He was successful in bringing individuals to the nets of Christ. He was not crowds driven. He was not stirring masses for Christ but he is the one who brought those who stir masses or crowds for Christ. Peter is the best example. Andrew is also someone who brings those that feed thousands. He brought the nameless boy whose resource pastored thousands (John 6:9). Producing open air preachers like Peter and committed pastors like the insignificant boy among the crowds (John 6: 9) that fed thousands was the call of Andrew. If one defines Andrew, Andrew is defined as the disciple of evangelization.

The Children of Zebedee

James and John were the other two brothers in Christ's squad. They were the children of Zebedee and they were Galileans. They were called from Galilee while they were fishing which details that they were professional fishermen while from where they got the fishing training is not known. But one argues that it was a business that they inherited and eventually got the training from their father who was also fishing around the Galilean see by the time James and John were called to follow Christ. As three of them including their father were running the fishing business, it is reliable to say that they had a fishing industry. The family had a boat, a net and professional fishing career.

James and John were a typical different group among the disciples. They were people rebuked for a wrong prayer longing for a position of hierarchy within Christ's squad according to Mark 10: 35-37. As they thought that Jesus was to establish an earthly kingdom, the children of Zebedee dreamt of taking the right and the left positions in Jesus' kingdom. This was a sign of seeking the highest position disregarding the other disciples. At the same time it was a planned manipulation of Christ through blood ties as their mother and Mary, the mother of Jesus were sisters. Accordingly, they were students engaging in nepotism where they were seeking everything good for themselves.

According to Arsim Gjinovic (2016, p. 421), nepotism is favoring relatives on the basis of family ties. Favoring here refers to all sorts of things that benefit the family members. It can be position, employment, financial benefit or anything that carries certain benefits towards the family member without the necessary qualification. James and John were favoring each other disregarding the other ten students of Christ. They were to have every benefit they assumed to be in the hands of the Zebedee children. They desired to be above the other disciples. In their call there was no above and subordinate status. All were equal. All had the same position in Christ. In a deviation from the Jesus way, the two students of Christ; James and John desired to be above all subordinating their co-followers of Christ.

Nepotism leads to conflict and internal security crisis. In the affirmation of this, the quest from James and John made the other ten disciples indignant. Jesus immediately rebuked their nepotistic approach by saying, "You do not know what you are asking," according to Mark 10: 38. Jesus also in strong terms renounced their quest to be above the others by saying, "Not so with you," in Mark 10: 43. The "Not so with you," was carrying the notion that this, such questions have no place in my presence and it is not what guides you. He then in a completely opposite understanding stated that whoever wants to be first among you must be the servant. Such places of servant hood are where one gains the "above status," and Jesus refuted the wrong prayer of the children of Zebedee. He also refuted the nepotism hidden in them.

They were also believed in a physical fight as a sign of revenging an opponent. They were enraged by anger and tried to call fire from heaven against the Samaritans. Revenge as a sign of raged character was among them while they were walking with a man who was resisting evil through compassion. Jesus then nicknamed them as the Boanerges; the children of Thunder in Mark 3: 17. Both James and John share similar traits as the students of Christ and the biological children of Zebedee but also possess differing features that will be discussed.

3. John

According to Dale Click (2000, p. 21) John was the younger brother of James and both were the children of Zebedee. Both were among the 1st four disciples to follow Christ and they were among the three nicknamed as the "Inner Circle." John, along with Peter and James, was named as the "Inner Circle" at large because these three disciples were at the key events with Jesus. No other disciple was close to Christ in major key events in Jesus' ministry and the way towards crucifixion.

The two brothers; John and James were obedient sons that contributed to their father's fishing industry to flourish. They were working with their father at a time they dropped everything and followed Christ. They were not in a position of failed business as failure may drag them to Christ. They were at work, not idiots sitting idle, proud professionals, and successful fishing men.

According to Mark Kern (2001, p. 886) fishing business in the 1st Century Palestine had a good income, equivalent to the upper middle class today. John along with his brother James abandoned this fishing business not as a failed business owner but as a called student sure of his future into the hands of Christ and taking Christ as the priority over everything.

Call

According to Pierson Parker (1962, p. 36) John was a Galilean by birth and it was from Galilee that he heard and answered Jesus' call (call (Matt 4 21; Mark 1 19; Luke 5:10). The terms "heard and answered," explain that there was a call and a response to it. The caller was Jesus and the responder was John. John's response was a response to hear and follow Christ abruptly. It was abrupt as there was no objection: John did not even say a word. He simply left everything and followed Jesus.

In describing John's abrupt decision to follow Christ, Iulian Faraoanu (2015, P 69) observes that it is a normal reaction to the irresistible presence of God. This irresistible presence of God was revealed in the person of Christ to which John's response was a "yes." The "yes" answer was a response to Jesus' divine calling power. The "yes" also carries with it the power and decision of abandoning everything and following Christ.

By abandoning ones belongings, to be a disciple takes to owning Christ. John abandoned his securities and found his different and un-perishing security; Jesus Himself for a life time and beyond. That was exactly what to be a student of Christ and discipleship is meant about. Faraoanu (2015, P 69) states that discipleship implies a definite answer: to leave everything and follow Christ. It is a free decision, the end of a lifestyle now belonging to the past.

Characters of John

Braveness:

Nelson Mandela quoted in the positivity project (2016) defined braveness as not the absence of fear but the power of overcoming it. Elaine L. Kinsella, Timothy D. Ritchie Saint, et al (2017, p. 2) defined braveness as the ability to confront danger or pain without fear. John exhibited this bravery in his walk with Christ as a student. First, he braved danger by entering the High Priest's residence during Christ's trial (John 18:15). His ability to enter the house, then to bring Peter in, means that John's family had access to the High Priest. Access to the High Priest's house was a symbol of bravery during the dangerous time. John was a true student of Christ who exposed himself to the highest danger a few hours before the crucifixion as a sign of bravery.

Second, when he joined Peter in the tomb, John saw the meaning of careful arrangement of grave clothes, and perspicaciously believed in Christ's resurrection (John 20:8-9). This spiritual insight may account for John's listing as second only to Peter when the apostles gathered in the Upper Room after Christ's ascension (Acts 1:13). John's entrance to the tomb also affirms his death and resurrection with Christ. It is also an affirmation of bravery as he did not afraid of the security guards and went into the tomb to make sure that his Master as He promised had left the cemetery. John then as an eyewitness to the empty tomb also became a witness to the resurrection. One cannot be a witness to the resurrection, without dying with Christ, without entering the tomb with Jesus, and without by faith declaring that Jesus was indeed raised from the dead. John was not only proved to be a firsthand witness to the resurrection, he was also a student who took forward the trumpet of speaking about the resurrected Christ to the world.

Violent Behavior:

John was a violent tempered disciple as he was to call fire from heaven on the Samaritans (Luke 9:54). John's violent behavior was restrained by Jesus and was rebuked and nicknamed "Sons of Thunder or Boanerges." Violence had no place in Jesus' ministry and He was against violence at any cost. Violence stems from hate. Hatred leads to violence against a certain group. That was why the two brothers were to call fire from heaven on the Samaritans.

Nepotism:

Added to having violent behavior as noted, John along with his brother James was also engaged in nepotism. Disregarding the other ten disciples, they were trying to manipulate Jesus' hand to get the right and the left side of Christ. They were seeking a special place for themselves leaving aside the other team members. This nepotistic behavior was because they knew that Mary the mother of Jesus and Salome; their mother were sisters and through blood ties they were to control Christ to get into the highest place of hierarchy. That is a typical example of selfishness. It was a typical example of an earthly mindset. Both James and John were selfish who were seeking self-glory for themselves through nepotism or a blood tie they had with Christ.

High Tempered & Intolerance:

John was a hair trigger tempered because of which he was named as, "Sons of Thunder," along with his brother James (Click 2000, p. 23). According to Pierson Parker (1962, p. 37) the phrase probably represents an Aramaic expression meaning "sons of wrath," i. e., wrathful and emotional men. This was because he was violent and outburst tempered who was not capable of controlling his temperament. To be a student of Christ cost his violent tempered behavior which attests a price tag attached to the love of Christ (p. 24).

John was also intolerant (Click 2000, p. 24) to those who are in the harvest filed of God. MacArthur (2003, p. 101) affirms that John was at times displaying an appalling intolerance. For example, in Luke 9: 49 John said, "We saw someone driving out demons in your name and we tried to stop him, because he is not one of us." Here, John was intolerant to those who were in the harvest field. He did not have accepting heart. John's taught was that only those who belong to his team participate in the ministry of the kingdom of God. He did not know that there were others who were commissioned for Christ. Jesus countered John's intolerant behavior saying, "Do not stop him," Jesus said, "For whoever is not against you is for you," in Luke 9: 50.

We are the only motive:
Besides intolerance, one argues that John was also obsessed with the notion that "We are the only," to be in this business. Such understanding stems from pride and undermining of others. Jesus was intolerant to this hidden pride motive and countered John's "we are the only," motive stating that you are not, "for whoever is not against you is for you." John thought that he and his groups were the only qualified but the qualifier downplayed the "We are the only qualified" notion welcoming the group that did not belong to the John's team but are in the harvest field as qualified, for they are not against Christ's kingdom.

In all, to be a student of Christ has a price tag; it costs us our pride, our intolerant behavior, our assumption of "we are the only," motive. In fact, John was not only a person obsessed with pride but also occupied with "unloving Spirit," as MacArthur (p. 101) writes. Unloving spirit is displayed in John when he was against a fellow believer who was not part of his team (Mark 9: 38). For John the group that is qualified as believers are only those "official members of the group," (p. 101) where the group refers to members of Christ's twelve disciples.

Glory without Suffering:
The doctrine of Christ attests that glory comes out of suffering. It means that the cross, suffering, and persecution leads to glory and it is not vice versa. There is no salvation without the cross. There is no life without death. In the school of Christ the cross is the ultimate

source of glory. The school of Christ is the way of the cross and each students of Christ is called to it without exemption. The cross is the mark of the students of Christ. Tim Chester (2009, p. 120) writes:

> The cross is the essential mark of Christian discipleship. We follow the way of the cross, not the way of glory. But we follow the way of the cross sustained by the hope of coming glory. The pattern of Christian experience conforms to the pattern of Christ's own experience. The way of the cross is followed by the glory of the resurrection. Suffering followed by glory.

While this doctrine is a guiding principle, according to MacArthur (2003, p. 111) "John was thirsty for glory and an aversion for suffering." MacArthur (p. 111) writes that "John's thirst for glory is seen in his desire for chief throne. John's aversion is observed in the fact that he forsook Jesus and fled on the night of His arrest" (Mark 14: 50). John did not know that the price tag attached to glory is suffering (MacArthur 2003, p.112) and indeed we suffer with Christ to be partakers of the heavenly glory with Him as Paul stated in Romans 8:17.

Earthly sufferings for the students of Christ are not an exemption, for it produces heavenly glory. In MacArthur's words (p. 112) Jesus taught His students this principle again and again. Then Jesus said to His disciples, "Whoever wants to be my disciple must deny themselves and take up their cross and follow me. For whoever wants to save their life will lose it, but whoever loses their life for me will find it (Matthew 16: 24-25). At last John learned the cost of glory in grieving the loss of his older brother James as the 1st martyr of the new church (p. 114).

John was also the only disciple who grieved the pain of the martyrdom of the entire disciples one by one (MacArthur, 2003, p. 114). John was left alone and that was the most painful of all (p.

114). John also suffered persecution and was put in jail in Turkey in Patmos in the Dodecanese Island where he wrote the apocalypse (P. 114). In all, John drank from the cup of suffering and proved to be a committed student of Christ until his death.

Interests

Exorcism: John among the students of Christ was interested in demon exorcism (Pierson Parker, 1962, p.40). According to Parker (p.40) John seems to have been on hand for every such healing that the Synoptic record (Matt 9:32; 12: 22; Mark 1:23, 32; 5 1; 7: 24; 9: 17; Luke 11:14). He was among those whom Jesus commissioned to cast out demons (Mark 3 15) and who were successful (Mark 6:13). On one occasion, when some of the disciples were not successful (Mark 9:17 f.), John was not among their number (p. 40). He was concerned that a person outside Jesus' band should not cast out demons in Jesus' name; and he, alone of the Twelve, took the matter up with his Master (Mark 9:38) (p.40). Thus the Apostle John was, if anything, more intensely concerned about demon exorcism than the others were (p.40).

To summarize, the power to cast out demons was a power given to the students of Christ. Matthew 10: 1 affirms: "Jesus called his twelve disciples to him and gave them authority to drive out impure spirits and to heal every disease and sickness." It is thus not a distinct gift to John as one of the students of Christ. While John might be more interested in exorcism, any student of Christ is given this authority and for that matter the power to cast out demons is only given to the students of Christ than anyone else.

Apocalyptic: John the son of Zebedee was, apparently, especially interested in apocalyptic (Parker, p.40). With his Galilean background, this was natural (p. 40). He was one of the two who asked about thrones in the Messiah's kingdom (Mark 10:35 f.), and one of three who asked about the signs that should presage the end

(Mark 13 3) (p. 40). The later question elicited from Jesus the final apocalyptic discourse (Matt. 24, 25; Mark 13; Luke 21 10 ff.) (p. 40).

Conclusion: Chosen for the divine mission from his Galilean fishing industry without his plan and his intention, John followed Christ due to the irresistible divine love. This love was a person; it was a person of Christ. John later detailed the theology of this love that won him for the everlasting kingdom. According to MacArthur (2003, p. 116) John's theology is best described as the theology of love. John, in a profound articulate way, explained to the world that God loved the world, loved His Son, and God is loved by Christ who loved His disciples, that all men love one another and love is the fulfillment of the law. Affirming this, Dwight Moody Smith (1995, p. 177) observes that love is in closed circle in John which Father, Son and believers participate mutually.

John detailed the saving work of Christ and clearly addressed to the world that Jesus is the one that gave sight to the blind. He is the light of the world as it is written in John 9. John also addressed to the world that Jesus is the life giving one as He brought back Lazarus to life in John 11. The theology here is not about the coming back to life of Lazarus but it pictures that Jesus is the only life giving now and in eternity. It is a depiction that whoever does not come to Jesus is already dead. John also presented that Jesus is the LOGOS- He is not the creature but He is one and the same being (homoousios) with the Father (Smith 1995, p. 175) through whom and in whom everything is created.

Jesus as a life giver, a creator and love is the one that called John and made him surrender to the call, live the call, and suffer for the call. John was also an ardent defender of the truth where the truth for John was Jesus Himself. John did not compromise over the truth and stood against sin, immorality and anti-Christian deceptions (MacArthur (2003, p. 116). John lived his uncommon calling bringing souls to the nets of Christ until the end of his life in around AD. 98 (p. 116-117) and then after through his contributions; the epistles and the gospel he provided to the world as an eye witness of Christ.

4. James

James is the older brother of John (MacArthur, 2003, p. 78) but little is known about him (p. 79). Although he is always mentioned after Peter in the lists of the disciples, he is not mentioned alone in many occasions. His name is always mentioned with his younger brother John except in the book of Acts where his martyrdom is recorded (p.77). At times they both are mentioned as the sons of Zebedee.

They are mentioned as "Sons of Zebedee" not without a reason (MacArthur, 2003, p. 77). First, it was because Zebedee was their Biological father. Second, it was because Zebedee was a known personality in Galilee. He had a fishing business where he hired many people (Click 2000, p. 21). It is also inferred that Zebedee hand financial success ((MacArthur 2003, p. 78). He was also a Levite (p. 78). This asserts that James came from a well to do family (Click 2000, p. 21).

James along with his brother John and Peter was also part of the inner circle (Click, 2000, p. 21). The "Inner Circle" refers to the presence of the three disciples; Peter, John and James with Christ in key events. James was present when Jesus raised Jairus daughter in Mark 5: 37. He was also with Jesus on the Mount of Transfiguration (Matthew 17: 1). He was also with Jesus on the Mount of Olives when Jesus unfolded the future to them (Mark. 13:3). James was also among the inner circles who were urged to pray privately in Gethsemane with Jesus (Mark 14: 33). He also saw the agony of Jesus in the garden during the crucifixion. From this, it is asserted that James' faith was strengthened leading him to be the first martyr for Christ.

The Call

James' call was not different either from his brother or the other members of the twelve especially Peter and Andrew. He was with one of the three disciples; Peter Andrew, and John when he abruptly responded to the divine call of Jesus (Matthew 4: 18–22).

As Jesus called him, James unquestionably, without uttering a word, abandoning his belongings including his father followed Christ. It was an unplanned decision but not emotion driven. It was a divine plan guided by a divine power to which James abruptly responded. In his response, James prioritized the call and took his final step to follow the Lord leaving his belongings.

James, like the other students of Christ, chose a life of poverty whereby he zeroed his economic, social and family ties for the sake of Christ. By choosing poverty, James proved that the life with Christ was a secured and unfailing call. He thus abandoned his fishing business, his boat, his net, his parents, and all that might have dragged him. For James and the entire squad of the students of Christ, Jesus was an incomparable eternal security who is chosen when even life looks unwinnable as one forsakes his/her life treasurers.

Description of James

Uncontrolled Behavior: According to Click (2000, p. 22) James' behavior was impulsive and quick tempered. His impulsive behavior was exposed when he was to call fire from heaven against the Samaritans. His imprudent behavior along with his brother John taped them with a nick name Boanerges in Mark 3: 17. John MacArthur (2003, p. 79) described James as bloodthirsty who would have ruined his life but transformed by the grace of God to be one of the leading students of Christ.

James along with his brother John had developed hate towards the Samaritans as the Samaritans were not racially pure Jews but mixed race (MacArthur 2003, p. 80). This may be taken as racial discrimination which Jesus did not tolerate as He refused James and John's quest of calling fire on the Samaritans. Added, the Samaritans worship was a mixture of paganism and the Jehovah as God accepting the five books of the Old Testament, the Pentateuch (p. 81-82). James and his brother John were also enraged by the hostile reception of Jesus by the Samaritans.

The Samaritans were generally considered unclean (MacArthur 2003, p. 82). They were mixed with races other than Jews and worshipped a pagan god mixed with the God of the Bible. Jesus was immune to this understanding that the Jews considered the Samaritans as unclean and He passed through Samaria. He healed a Samaritan leprosy (Luke 17: 16) and received water from a Samaritan woman and gave her the water of life (John 4: 7–29). Jesus also made the best parable on the Samaritans (Luke 10: 30-37) and commanded His disciples to preach the Gospel in Samaria. Jesus was not bound to traditions and He was not trapped because of people's uncleanness or religious background. Jesus always touched the unclean, break cultural barriers and reached to those segregated. Jesus thus rebuked James and John against their hatred towards the Samaritans.

Nepotistic Behavior: He was nepotistic as he was seeking great advantage from Christ excluding the other students of Christ. Jesus countered James' nepotistic move to be tapped with an appointment to the right and the left of Christ. Jesus countered by giving a unique lesson that whoever wants to be great must choose the position of a slave. According to MacArthur (2003, p. 91) James wanted to have a crown of glory from a nepotistic feeling which Jesus countered by giving him a cup of suffering as Jesus stated, "Are you able to drink the cup that I drink?" in Matthew 20:22. James also sought power but Jesus gave him servant hood (P. 91). He also sought prominence among the twelve but Jesus tapped him with martyrs' grave which he faced when he was killed for Christ later in Acts 12: 1–3 (p, 91).

Seeking Glory without suffering:
James was an ambitious student of Christ to have glory without suffering. The theology of Christ was that out of the cross glory comes, out of suffering glory pores and it was not vice versa. Jesus was equipping His students to the doctrine of the cross, suffering, persecution and death out of which glory comes. According to MacArthur (2003, p. 91) James was against this as he wanted a

crown of glory, a crown of power, a place of prominence and wanted to rule.

In summary, MacArthur (p. 91) writes that Jesus countered James by giving him the cup of suffering out of which glory comes. Instead of power that James was seeking, Christ gave James servant hood. James sought to rule but Jesus gave him a sword to be an instrument of execution. James sought a place of prominence but Jesus gave him a martyr's grave. In affirmation of this, James became the 1st of all the students of Christ to be killed and whose actual history of death is recorded (p. 92).

Boanerges:

The name was given to both John and James to describe their violent behavior. James' personality in vivid terms was Boanrges because James was truly zealous, thunderous, passionate and fervent (MacArthur (p. 79). This type of behavior is bloodthirsty in the same way as Jehu's behavior (2kings 9:20; 2 kings 10:31) in the Old Testament (p. 79).

Jehu had a mixed behavior of selfishness, uncontrolled zeal for the Lord, and a heart that did not depart from sin (MacArthur, p. 79). Such behavior filled with zeal is always wrong as it turns out deadly. It needs to be guided by knowledge, wisdom (p. 80), and handled with care. Jesus transformed James' behavior by his grace for His kingdom.

Empowered by the Holy Spirit, James became true Boanerges for Christ's kingdom. His zeal, ambition and passion became useful instruments for spreading the kingdom of God (MacArthur P.93). James apparently used his zealous, passionate and ambitious qualities for the Lord's service other than for self-aggrandizement (P. 93) giving his life as a first martyr among the students of Christ.

Boanerges depicts that the children of Zebedee (John and James) proved to be a true force- a thunder for the Gospel of Christ. Boanerges became a lighting force that cracks the forces of evil with the word of God, a lighting force that silences evil in compassion, a lighting force that stands firm for truth in front of death and a lighting force that drinks the cup of suffering for the coming glory.

Conclusion: James was a student controlled by a wrong zeal, "Boanerges," but this wrong zeal was transformed into a zeal for the expansion of the kingdom of God. "Boanerges," became an instrument not for hate but for breaking boundaries to reach to the other races for the gospel. A once hate controlled person; James was given the message of love to go to the world and preach. The world signifies the possibility of crossing languages, racial groups, cultures and religious communities. To reach to the other racial groups beyond one's race is possible only if the students of Christ are compassionate towards every race, language and culture. It is only possible when we are a thundering force for Christ. .

The Gospel of Christ is for every race and that mission of reaching is a mission assigned to the students/the disciples of Christ. This mission carries with it a cup of suffering to which the students of Christ are called. James took this cup of suffering and honorably gave his life for martyrdom keeping his answer to the question of Christ in Matthew 20:22.

James was at last able to control his passion, his anger, and revenge guided emotions. He was able to pass through sufferings and became a marvelous instrument of God in front of King Herod Agrippa who killed him with a sword (Acts 12: 2). He selflessly gave his life for Christ echoing his words that he said to Jesus in Matthew 10: 38–39, "Jesus said. "Can you drink the cup I drink or be baptized with the baptism I am baptized with?" [39] "We can," they answered.

In fact, James printed his name in history books as the first martyrdom of a young church in AD 44 (William S. McBirnie 2008, p. 26). James also proved to be a forgiving person filled with love by forgiving Clement of Alexandria who passed the judgment verdict of the killing of James (MacArthur 2003, p. 93). James forgave Clement who finally was beheaded with him accepting Christ as his savior but a striking fact was that James proved to be a soul winner even at a time to give his life for execution for the glory of God.

5. Matthew

Unlike the other disciples, Matthew was a tax collector. He was an employee of the Romans and in charge of collecting taxes. There is no evidence available as long as where he got the training to complete his careers in taxation. It can only be argued that Matthew grasped some form of taxation training from the Romans or from any school available at that time. This asserts that Matthew was literate.

As a tax collector, he was collecting dues and customs from persons and goods crossing the Sea of Galilee, or passing along the great Damascus road which ran along the shore between Bethsaida, Julius and Capernaum (Harold Willington, 1999). Christ called him from this work to be His disciple. He appears to have been a man of wealth, for he made a great feast in his own house, perhaps in order to introduce his former companions and friends to Jesus (Willington, 1999). His business would tend to give him knowledge of human nature, and accurate business habits, and of how to make a way to the hearts of many publicans and sinners not otherwise easily reached (Willington, 1999).

The only credentials (MacArthur 2000, p. 150) he has before being the disciple of Christ was collecting taxes. His taxation career was one of the most hated careers among the Jewish and he was considered as a notorious sinner than any among the twelve (p. 151). MacArthur (2000, p. 153) writes:

> Tax collectors are socially harlots (Matthew 21:32) and it was worse for the Jewish man like Matthew to be a tax collector. His occupation made him a traitor to the nation, social pariah, and the rankest of the

rank. He would also have been a religious outcast, forbidden to enter any synagogue.

This notion asserts that "Matthew's friends (MacArthur 2000, p. 153) were the riffraff of the society, petty criminals, hoodlums, prostitutes, and their ilk."

Call

Matthew was also called Levi but unlike Peter, it is doubted if the name Matthew was given to him by Jesus. Matthew is a Greek name and Levi is the Jewish name. Matthew means the gift of Jehovah. It is derived from a Hebrew name "Matthias," which means the "gift of Jehovah," as in Acts 1: 23. Except for language differences and how the two names are pronounced both Matthew and Matthias are the same in meaning, depicting that the name was not given by Jesus. He is the "son of Alpheus," according to Mark 2:14. Luke also supports this in Luke 5: 27–29. But in two other places Luke calls him as Matthew in Luke 6: 15 and Acts 1: 13.

The call of Matthew was the most astounding of the call (Matthew 9: 9). What is astounding is not his abrupt calling as the same applies to the other disciples, but the truth that the most notorious sinner, the most disliked person, outcast among the Jewish was trapped into the call of Christ. The power of Christ's grace surpasses human traditions and human sinfulness, even drags those who are outcast and horrible sinners to be His lifetime students.

The case of Matthew, the most disliked, a man who was considered as an enemy to his nation for working for the Romans and surrounded by the outcast sinners explicitly describes the infinite love of Christ that calls those outcasts to the kingdom of God. This infinite love of God was even exhibited in Jesus sitting with those outcast people and Matthew at a banquet prepared in Matthew's house (Matthew 9: 10).

According to Matthew 9: 10ff, Matthew invited so many people;

the outcast to be introduced to Christ. While we do not have any clue of how many were surrendered to Christ, this chapter states that Jesus was the most important person; a life giver to the outcast, to those who are on the wrong side of history, to those who are historically marginalized, the ones beyond no return because of their sin, the harlots of the society, the low life, and that was why Matthew invited them. Matthew knew for sure that Jesus is the lover of the social harlots, the segregated, the discriminated, the outcast and the low life.

Matthew, as he abruptly followed Jesus, according to MacArthur (2000, p. 155) "he instantly and without hesitation arose and followed Jesus abandoning his tax office and abandoning his "cursed profession" forever." The instant and without hesitation as discussed earlier vividly depict the divine power of the call of Jesus. "Cursed profession" though is contextual as there is no cursed profession unless it is something that affects one's morality and degrades the value of someone into an object. The best example for this is prostitution. Melissa Farley (2017, p. 100-101) quoting Sharp describes Prostitution as:

> The sale of a sex act or the exchange of a sex act for goods such as food, shelter… for such a sale or exchange to occur, there must be an objectified, dehumanized, and commodified class of women,…. Commodification requires objectification, a process that transforms people into objects with economic value.

MacArthur (2000, p. 155) states that Matthew's decision was irreversible and once he got out of the tax office someone grasps his position as it is the money center where one has access to money. Matthew left his career without knowing what the future holds for him (p. 155). He left his security and his livelihood security status into the hands of the unfailing Jesus. Matthew's irreversible decision was only because the divine power of Jesus trapped him forever.

In general, from his abrupt calling, he did not even give a second thought (MacArthur (2000, p. 157) of the reason he abandoned everything but remained as a profound Gospel writer among the twelve, preached Christ and finally martyred for Jesus. MacArthur (p. 157) writes that Matthew remained to give his all for Christ to the very end affirming what the cost of studentship is meant about.

Description of Matthew:

Matthew came from one of the most despised backgrounds among the Jewish community of the time of Christ (Got Questions, 2015). It was because he was working for the Roman government which was taken as a sign of high security breach as he was working for an enemy. That means Matthew was standing against the interest of his own people. Also, as Matthew was enriching himself through dishonestly collecting excessive amounts of money from the tax collection (Got Questions, 2015) he was considered as unclean. He was thus seen as an unforgivable sinner among the Jewish.

As a tax collector, it was surmised that he got some form of training in taxation. That concludes that Matthew was in a better economic condition. His career also puts him in a completely different personality among the students of Christ whose background was mostly in a fishing industry. Matthew was exposed to some form of writing and accounting skills (Got Questions, 2015). Based on his writing from the gospel of Matthew, one also concludes that Matthew had a profound knowledge of the person of Christ after he became the student of Christ.

A writer: Matthew was one of the few students of Christ that produced a big volume of book on Christ and gave it the world--- the Gospel According to Matthew. According to Got Questions (2015) Matthew wrote the gospel with the intention "to prove to the Jews that Jesus Christ is the promised Messiah." Got Questions (2015) writes to back up its argument stating that Matthew:

> Quotes the Old Testament to show how Jesus fulfilled the words of the Jewish prophets. Matthew describes in detail the lineage of Jesus from David, and uses many forms of speech that Jews would have been comfortable with. Matthew's love and concern for his people is apparent through his meticulous approach to telling the gospel story.

John Nolland states that (2005, p. 38-39) Matthew did not give up the Jewish tradition in favor of the new one but was presenting the decisive acts of God in history to which his Jewish people were acquainted. According to Nolland (p. 42) the Jewish people were the children of God and now Mathew writes Jesus as the son of God the same way as the Israelites were. Jesus is the son of God as the messiah is the son of God in clearly presenting Jesus as the savior of the Jewish people and the promised messiah. In this case one writes that Matthew was effective in contextualizing Jesus to his Jewish audience.

Matthew's blending of the New Testament Christ into the Jewish belief system was by far a contextualization that used points of contacts within the Jewish religion and the words of Jesus, as one of the Jews to prove to the Jewish that Jesus was the promised Messiah.

Conclusion:

Matthew's call passes the message to the world that Jesus always loves those who are the notorious sinners. He calls them to His everlasting kingdom and washes them to be the instruments of His purpose. Those who are at odds to the society in their behavior, character, and manner and considered evil are loved by Jesus. The Matthew's Jesus is the Jesus that takes away all unwanted behaviors, washes them and uses those who are unthinkable for His glory.

6. The nationalist, Simon the Zealot

Simon the Zealot was among the little known in Christ's squad. Except his appointment as a student among the twelve, less is known about him. To begin with, Simon was called the Zealot in Luke 6: 15 but in Matthew 10: 4 and Mark 3: 18 he was named as Simon the Cananite. This does not mean there is a discrepancy in meaning. According to MacArthur (2000, p. 174) "Cananite is not a reference to the village of Canaan or the village of Cana but it comes from the Hebrew root qanna, which means to be Zealous." This notion asserts that there is no difference between Simon the Zealot and Simon the Cananite.

Zealot refers to a political party to which Simon was a member. According to MacArthur (2000, p. 175) the Zealots were an outlawed political organization among the Jews and they hated the Romans and their goal was to overthrow the Roman occupation. The Zealots were expecting the Messiah who would lead them in ending the Roman rule. In this case, Simon as a pro- Jewish State was at the opposite of Matthew.

Matthew was an employee of the Roman government; he had the most hated career; tax collecting. The Jewish, including Simon the Zealot, do not want to see the Roman occupation and were against those working for the Romans. It is thus asserted from this that Matthew and Simon the Zealot; the terrorist according to MacArthur (p. 175) were in two different antagonistic camps. These camps were the Romans' camp as the oppressor and the Jewish camps as the oppressed.

Matthew was working for the oppressors and Simon was working to topple the Romans from the oppressed. At one point according to MacArthur (p.177) Simon could have gladly killed Matthew. Also, as Jesus was talking about His ultimate death than a Messiah who would liberate the Jewish from the Roman over lordship, "some might have expected Simon to be a betrayer"(p. 177) who surrenders Jesus to the Jewish.

Jesus as a soul winner and as the one who calls the unthinkable from life extremes to be His students divinely called both Matthew and Simon the Zealot. Both had extremely dangerous lives. Both were notorious sinners trapped into the divine call of Christ. Simon, the Zealot defying the expectations of some did not list his name as a traitor but printed his name as a convicted loyal zealous student of Christ who embraced Christ as his personal Lord (MacArthurP. 177). Simon also was made a true brother with Matthew; a partner of the Gospel (P.177) embracing the Great Commission of Christ in Matthew 28: 18–20.

Conclusion: Despite the scanty presence of information about what happened to Simon the Zealot, according to MacArthur (2000, p. 178), Simon took the Gospel of Christ North ward and preached in the British Isles. As a transformed disciple who abandoned his early political passions and affiliation to the Zealots, he proved to be a loyal committed student of Christ who joined the martyrs of the Gospel in "giving his life" (p. 178) for the cause of the Gospel.

7. Nathanael

Was a Galilean native like the other ten students (John 21: 2) of Christ. He is barely mentioned in the gospel for the reason that is unclear. He is almost completely absent in the synoptic to describe him fully. The only place he was mentioned by the synoptic writers was in the list of the disciples. The synoptic writers call him Bartholomew. John is the only writer who calls him Nathanael and mentions him in two places. These two places are at his beginning as a disciple and after the resurrection of Christ. They are in John 1 where his call is recorded and John 21: 2 where he was mentioned among the returnees to Galilee after the resurrection of Christ.

Nathanael perfectly knew his beginning and his place to return even when the worst things happen in life. At the time when Jesus was betrayed and finally nailed on the cross as a criminal and put in the grave as if he would not come back, Nathanael along with the scattered disciples did not give up. He came back to Christ as the resurrection of Christ was assured silencing death forever. He was not emotion driven to come and emotion driven to go. He was a stable minded who knew that Christ is the priority in life.

Call

Nathanael was a Galilean from insignificant place but the most important in the ministry of Jesus; Cana. Cana is insignificant as it is barely mentioned in the Bible. It was significant because it was where Jesus exhibited His glory as a Messiah, as a Living word, as an alternative wine than a mere wine from the Canaan village (John 2: 1–12). The alternative life giving wine in Cana trapped Nathanael to be His student for a life time. It is also logical to argue that from the insignificant places, God is always calling people. The ghettos, the unknowns, the obscured places of the world are where God calls His people. It does not mean other places are not important in the mission of God's calling power.

One amazing feature in the call of Nathanael was how Jesus depicted his character. A man in whom there was no deceit (John 1: 47) was a word that came out of Jesus at the onset of the call of Nathanael to be a life time student. Jesus clearly depicted the history of Nathanael as a person without deceit, a true Israelite unlike the history of most people, especially the good things they did comes during their funeral (MacArthur 2000, p.143).

"A true Israelite" does not mean the genetic makeup, Jesus was referring that Nathanael was a true offspring of Abraham who was worshiping the true living God (MacArthur 2000, p.143). Nathanael became a true disciple of Christ from the start (p. 143). Studentship in Christ begins upon the call and continuously grows. Both the call and being the disciple of Christ are automatic divine occurrences in the believer. The popular perception is that one becomes a disciple sometimes after he comes to Christ but the call of Nathanael and for that matter the whole doctrine of Christ disproves that. One becomes the disciple of Christ immediately and grows in discipleship as he / she walks with Christ.

A call from the "Under Fig Tree"

Nathanael means "God has given." It is a name referencing God as a giver where it means that Nathanael was a gift from God for his families. In the synoptic, Nathanael was mentioned as Bartholomew which is a Hebrew surname "Son of Tolami." This infers that Nathanael was the son of Tolami or Nathanael Bar-Tomei. Thus, it is not two separate names given to the same person but one unlike Peter who had two separate names; Peter & Simon.

As depicted in John (John 1: 45–49), Nathanael was brought to Christ by his friend Philip, one of the disciples. The notion that Philip brought him to Christ explains that Jesus was a uniquely important person in the life of Philip and for this reason Philip was directing others to Christ. With this convection and faith, Philip was sure that Jesus is the most important, the life giver for his friend; Nathanael.

As he came to Jesus Nathanael began questioning the credibility of Jesus as the Messiah that Philip dictated he found. Nathanael's question began in John 1:48 with a simple question, "How do you know me?" According to MacArthur (2000, p. 144) Nathanael was not prone to skepticism nor questioning the scripture about the Messiah but he did not get the picture that a Messiah comes from Nazareth, a town completely absent in the Old Testament. MacArthur (p. 144) farther details that the question of Nathanael was because Jesus was the son of a carpenter, a no name and non-descript man from a town which had no prophetic connection in the Old Testament. This states that for Jesus to be the right Messiah, Jesus has to have a big name, a big profession and from affluent or probably from a well-known town of the Old Testament possibly attached to prophetic words. Jesus then countered this understanding of Nathanael by explicitly speaking that He knew him before Philip and when Nathanael was under the "Fig Tree," (John 1: 48). This word out of the mouth of Jesus challenged Nathanael as it prints in the mind of Nathanael that someone with omniscient and omnipresent power was present near him and sees him. Nathanael's entire life was under a divine microscope where that divine power is right beside him; Jesus of Nazareth. But why was Nathanael under a fig tree?

A fig tree or any tree is used as a shade (MacArthur, 2000, P.145). That means it is used as a place to escape from hot weather (P. 145). A fig tree also provides fruits. That means it is a source of food. It is a place where one escapes from a stifling atmosphere of a house (P.145). That means it is a protection. Fig trees are also used as a place of privacy, study and reflection. Jesus, by pointing the place of Nathanael as a fig tree, is presenting Himself as an alternative place of rest, a protection, and an everlasting bread of life and a private gift of life. In doing so, Jesus detached Nathanael from his "private chamber" according to MacArthur (p. 145).

The "private chamber" of Nathanael, the "fig tree," was everything. As noted, it is a protection, a source of food and a place of rest. Nathanael could not know that Jesus was a good shepherd, an eternal food from heaven and an eternal resting place. Jesus was a refuge who was hovering over Nathanael and protecting him even when Nathanael did not recognize. As a good shepherd; Jesus revealed himself as undying, eternal, a source of heavenly food and a permanent resting place. Nathanael then beyond his questions falls into the trap of the studentship of Christ prophesying "Rabbi, you are the Son of God; you are the king of Israel," as in John 1:49.

By declaring Jesus as the King and the son of God; a true essence of God, Nathanael got the true deity of Christ. His knowledge of the Old Testament from Psalms 2 to Zephaniahs 3: 15 where the scripture depicted the messiah as the king of Israel assured him that the king, the messiah is right here beside him. Jesus then stated to Nathanael that more is yet to come. Your growth far above this is beginning. An astounding feature of Nathanael's theology was that at a time when the person who brought him to Christ Philip did not recognize who Jesus was to the end, Nathanael's studentship began with a profound understanding of Christ.

Conclusion: The call of Nathanael attests that wherever we are, we are under divine microscope and nothing is hidden from Christ. Jesus' divine power is not masked by geography nor the human heart. Jesus sees us anywhere and reads our hearts. While Nathanael did not recognize, Jesus was in control of Nathanael's environment and heart. The same Lord today calls people to be His students and anyone's call is a miracle as Jesus drags us to Himself controlling our environments and reading our hidden hearts.

8. Judas, the son of James

Judas was listed as the second to the last among the faithful disciples followed by Judas Iscariot. The name Judas beyond its meaning which means "Jehovah leads" connotes a negative understanding due to the treachery that Judas Iscariot played in the betrayal of Christ (Click 200, p. 43). In John 14:22 Judas, the son of James, was named as Judas to differentiate him from Judas Iscariot. In the synoptic he was named as Lebbaeus and Thaddaeus. Judas the son of James was named by all these names in part but synonymous to John to distinguish him from Judas Iscariot or to completely avoid a name attached to someone who denied and completely abandoned Jesus Christ.

Click observes (2000, p. 43) that Judas the son of James had three different names and he was referred by three of them at different occasions most probably to distinguish him from the betrayer. He had three different names and Jerome called him Trinomios according to MacArthur (2003, p. 178). Trinomios means three. Click (2000, p. 43) states that to have three names was not uncommon in those days but the only among the twelve to have three names. These three names are:

a. **Judas:** MacArthur (2003, p. 178) writes that Judas was probably the name given to him at birth. It is inferred from this that to be sure of the name Judas as if it was given by his parents remains a subject of further research.

b. **Lebbaeus:** This name is mentioned in Matthew 10: 3 and possibly a nickname. It was not a name given by Christ when he was called but it has special significance as one infers from its meaning as stated by MacArthur (p.178). It is a name whose root is heart and thus Judas was a "heart child." This depicts that Judas was one of the most loved among the family. He was dependable and trusted. Judas, as a person with a childlike heart, wanted to know how Jesus manifests Himself to him and his colleagues than the world in John 14: 21. Judas was thinking in a worldly mentality that Jesus will be the ruler of the world. Judas thought that Jesus will be forming a political realm where He is ruling but Jesus answered in explicit terms in John 14: 23 saying, "Anyone who loves me will obey my teaching. My Father will love them, and we will come to them and make our home with them." This question was not generated from Judas ambition to have different motives to have a special place in the kingdom he imagined in his brain like the children of Zebedee. The question was generated from a compassionate heart. Such hearts were also what Jesus was looking for.

Jesus was all rounded in seeking hearts. He was seeking the most notorious hearts like that of Matthew, He was seeking the most political and terrorist minds like that of Simon the Zealots. All hearts are attracted to Jesus through His divine magnetic power. The most extreme hearts, the most extremely dangerously hated moral standards of the prostitutes are attracted by Christ.

c. **Thaddaeus** means breast child according to MacArthur (2003, p. 178). "Breast child," was used to distinguish from a nursing baby according to MacArthur (p. 178) but to depict that he was one of the most loved and possibly the youngest in the family and among the twelve (p. 178). In all, the nick names exemplify that Judas, the son of James had a childlike heart (p. 178); He had a pure heart, a compassionate and loving heart. Click (2000, p. 43) observes that Judas the son of James was also a nationalist which MacArthur (2003, p. 178) disagrees based on the notion that Judas the son of James had a soul hanging heart than that of Simon the Zealot. Click (p.43) states that both Judas the son of James and Simon the zealot were listed among the last four partly because they possess nationalistic –Zealous feelings. One may argue that "to have a soul hanging heart, a loving heart, a compassionate heart" never evokes someone from becoming a nationalist. Similarly, unlike Click (p. 43) to be listed among the last four of the twelve students of Christ assumed to have similar Characters does not make Judas the son of James to be a nationalist.

A conclusion can be drawn that Jesus' eternal divine love attracts people of diverse back ground into His kingdom. It is not peoples' past or present what matters but the divine calling power of God. This divine calling power calls the harlots, the prostitutes, the dangerous sinners and others into the everlasting kingdom to be the students for the divine mission.

According to MacArthur (2003, p. 179) Judas the son of James had only one time verbal contact recorded in the scripture (John 14: 21) but he was proved to be one of the loyal students. He betrayed Christ like all the twelve but he did not give up. He came back to Christ after Christ resurrected and finally according to history went to Edessa, a city of North Mesopotamia in Turkey (Click, 2000, p 43–44; MacArthur, p. 179). It is recorded that Judas the son of James had healing gifts and healed many people from their sickness in this place but finally killed in Ararat for the gospel and committed himself for Christ as a faithful student to the end (Click, 2000, p 43-44; MacArthur (p. 179).

Conclusion: As one sees from the scripture (John 14:21), Judas verbal utterance is only in one place. This teaches us that God has so many people on the planet that have no records of themselves, nor publicly spoken records of Christ. Humans always think that those who have recorded history of what they did or said are better off but Judas history teaches us that Jesus have those unseen, unnoticed remnants with no record of talk or did but sacrificed themselves for the gospel.

9. Thomas

Thomas also called "Didymus," according to John 11:16 is an apostle whose history is limited to Theologians because he was mentioned only once in each synoptic gospels but whatever is available about who he is came out of the gospel of John. "Didymus," means twin in Greek and it was probably because he had a twin brother or sister. It can also be argued that Didymus was given to him because he has a kind of double life standard. He is one of the twelve who committed himself for Christ but unlike that according to MacArthur, (2003, p. 161) he was a pessimist who was always looking the darkest side of something.

Thomas was not positive. He was always expecting the worst out of the situations and thus described as pessimist (MacArthur 2003, p. 161). For example, according to John 11: 16: Then Thomas also known as Didymus said to the rest of the disciples, "Let us also go, that we may die with him." MacArthur (p, 161) describes this as pessimism and in fact as "heroic pessimism."

"Heroic pessimism," is the courage to take the worst case senior in life and Thomas was determined to take that and even to die as he stated that he may go and die. Two things play out here. First, he was so courageous but his courage was to cause a disaster. It was courage for bad. He did not have faith in the Lord that Jesus changes the situation into an opportunity. The courage of Thomas was thus courage of lacking trust in the Lord in the worst situations. He always sees darkness through the situations and he was ready to accept it.

On the other hand, the lifestyle of Didymus depicts that he was the follower of Jesus who was called to place his trust in his Lord in whatever situation other than seeing and expecting bad out of situations. Because he had both lifestyles; a life of trust and un-trust; Didymus was a person of double standard life. A life of trust takes us to the notion below.

Second, beyond MacArthur's assertion of "heroic pessimism," how about if it shows commitment to Christ as Thomas asserted "Let us also go, that we may die with him." Beyond pessimism thus optimism, it proves that Thomas was committed to Christ and he had the courage to take any action to the extent of giving his life. It asserts that Thomas' love for Christ was beyond situations and even in the darkest moments of life. He was a determined disciple amidst the risk that Jesus would be stoned to death as stated in John 8:59 & 10:31.

Thomas was rallying the other disciples to go to Jerusalem but they did not (Click, 2000, p. 34–35). It proves that Thomas was committed and determined to go to the town where Jesus was paying the ultimate price for sin (p. 35). Thomas was a person committed to go and see the last supper, the crucifixion whatever it cost and determined to go to Jerusalem (p. 35). This understanding counters the notion that Thomas was a doubter. He may have doubted like anyone of us but he was a student who believes in investigation, he was a student of data, facts and a student who questions to believe (Click, 2000, p. 33).

Depending on data or investigation does not always mean doubt. It leads to fact findings. Investigation is done to reach a conclusion that leads to true findings beyond suspicious conclusion or doubt or assumptions.

Thomas was looking for truth but truth is not always reached through investigation or even facts but it comes through faith in Christ. Thomas, beyond his logic and reason filled brain could have stuck to Christ in faith. In all, there was doubt in Thomas, he was seeking the truth and that was not wrong but Thomas could have stuck his mind and spirit to Christ in faith. In general, Thomas could not be taken as a doubter in entirety.

Added to the assertions above, Thomas had different features as a student of Christ. He was someone who was left alone after Jesus was crucified. He was a lone fighter amidst life crises, devastations and life difficulties. As Jesus was crucified when all the disciples went their ways Thomas went his own ways. But as the disciples gathered in the upper room to comfort each other, Thomas was absent. He was fighting all his sorrows by himself (MacArthur, p.116). His loneliness in sorrows, life difficulties cost him that he was not there among the students of Christ when Jesus entered the closed room and transformed the disciples' heavy sadness into joy according to John 20: 19-20, 24–25:

> On the evening of that first day of the week, when the disciples were together, with the doors locked for fear of the Jewish leaders, Jesus came and stood among them and said, "Peace be with you!" After he said this, he showed them his hands and side. The disciples were overjoyed when they saw the Lord… Now Thomas (also known as Didymus), one of the Twelve, was not with the disciples when Jesus came. So the other disciples told him, "We have seen the Lord…!

Besides his absence from the upper room, Thomas did not believe when he heard that Jesus was raised from the dead. He doubted and thus considered as a pessimist. John 20: 25 describes this incident as follows:

So the other disciples told him, "We have seen the Lord!"
But he said to them, "Unless I see the nail marks in
his hands and put my finger where the nails were,
and put my hand into his side, I will not believe.

Thomas was not a doubter at first. He followed Jesus without
any hesitation at the beginning, but latter doubted as he heard the
resurrection of Christ. Taking the benefits of the doubt though
Thomas looks one of the most intelligent in not depending on people's
experience of Christ than his own. He rejected the experience of the
disciples in its entirety (John 20: 25). He did not want to accept their
witness. He was someone who depended on the personal experience
of Christ than what friends reported to him about the resurrection
of Christ. He then after experimenting believed in the resurrected
Jesus and declared in John 20:28 "My Lord and my God," the best
creed ever confessed (Click 2000, p. 33).

Conclusion: Thomas had one of the most fascinating characters
among the twelve. He was a pessimist but also a determined person
committed to the love of Christ to accept anything including
death. He was a lone fighter who believes in experiments about the
resurrection of Christ through reason and proof which elaborates
that he was Dedymus; the actual doubter but beyond doubt accepts
the truth from the heart and declares Jesus as His lord and His God.
Like the twelve, Thomas was believed to take the gospel to India and
killed there for Christ (MacArthur, 2003, p. 164) as the ultimate call
to true studentship of Christ.

10. Philip

According to MacArthur (2003, p. 119) the name Philip is a Greek
name, meaning "lover of horses." No one knows why this name was
given to him and no one knows if he had a Jewish name as he was a

Jew. MacArthur (2003, p. 119) states that Philip had a Greek name probably because his parents were from Hellenistic Jews. It may also be stated that probably Philip loves riding horse. Philip, a Galilean by birth, was from the town of Bethsaida (John 1: 44). Click (2000, p. 27) supports this notion asserting that Philip was from Bethsaida, the home of Peter and Andrew. Click (p. 27) also notes that Philip the disciple should not be confused with Philip in the book of Acts 6:5. They are completely different individuals but had the same name.

Philip had a close relationship with the four disciples; the key players in the squad; Peter, Andrew, James and John who were all from Galilee and the town of Bethsaida. The notion that they were all from the same place avows that they were probably friends, boys of the same town who influenced each other to have the same career and to come to Christ (MacArthur 2003, p. 120). Thus, MacArthur (p. 120) explains that Philip was a fisherman. His fishing career was probably shaped by his friends or his fishing career shaped his friends. They were all coworkers, had the same occupation, be friended to each other as people of the same small town (p.120). The best Biblical evidence that supports this notion is John 21:3 where Peter stated, "I am going fishing." The other disciples immediately said, "We are going with you also." MacArthur (p. 120) writes that these group included Thomas, Peter, Nathanael, and the sons of the Zebedee and two other unnamed disciples. These unnamed disciples in the words of MacArthur (p. 120) were Philip and Andrew.

The idea that Jesus gathered people of the same background, same occupation, and same place of origin does not mean Jesus was not drawn to diversity. These groups, unlike their similarities, are too diverse in personality, understanding, commitment, and even post Jesus resurrection mission. When it comes to their personality as stated in Chapter three they were completely different people from the outspoken Peter to the children of Zebedee who were engaging in nepotism and from Thomas, one of the most intelligent student of Christ who depended on data and experiment to the notorious sinner Matthew are completely diverse groups. From the committed politician Simon the Zealot to Judas the son of James who possessed a Childlike heart and the materialistic Judas Iscariot to Nathanael who was questioning Christ were all diverse groups with different gifts and talents.

The students of Christ were different groups whose success never depended on them but on the one who called them from insignificant towns like Cana to the Galilean village. They were all called not because of their exceptional talents but because Jesus' divine power made them, "They will do," as MacArthur (2003, p. 121) writes. MacArthur (2003, p. 121) notes that what matters was their availability and that was what Jesus used to train them, shape them, make them missional and built them.

The Call of Philip

Philip was called immediately after the 1st four disciples Peter, Andrew, John and James. What connects all of them was the divine calling power of Christ. The 1st were called from their fishing career according to the synoptic gospel but John addresses as if they were directed to Jesus by John the Baptist while they were in the wilderness according to the gospel of John. A wilderness is not a place to be chosen. It is a place of harsh climate and scanty resources but it was from here that Jesus called his 1st four disciples according to John.

The disciples went to the wilderness to hear John the Baptist that propelled their heart for the coming Messiah. MacArthur (2003, p. 122) asserts that the disciples had a seeking heart; a heart that is looking for the kingdom of God. This, as MacArthur (2003, p. 122) writes attest that God is sovereignly drawing the disciples to Himself. Those in the wilderness have some sort of vacuum and they always need something to fill their vacuum. They are thirsty for something or someone to fill the void spaces of their heart. They are seekers. That seeking heart needs to recognize that God is knocking the heart to win for eternity and make a lifelong student.

A life without Christ is a life in the wilderness and Jesus is always drawn to those who are in the wilderness. Philip was also here before he left to Galilee where he was trapped into the everlasting net of Christ. MacArthur (2003, p. 122) cautiously expresses that the 1st four disciples were the one who found Jesus but it is theologically disputed as Jesus was the one who called them. That does not yet contradict the notion that someone came or comes to Christ through someone else. In this regard, John's description of the 1st four disciples to be directed to Christ does not contradict the notion that Jesus found them. In both cases, Jesus is the one who attracts people into Himself by His divine magnetic power. John 6:44 affirms, "No one can come to me unless the Father who sent me draws them, and I will raise them up at the last day."

The Synoptic gospel writers articulately put that Jesus called the 1st four disciples while they were fishing in the Galilean Sea. The disciples astounding yes to the call with their exceptional abandoning of their livelihoods, securities to follow Christ affirm the divine calling power of Christ. This divine calling power was the one that trapped Philip for eternity.

Philip stated that he found Jesus in John 1: 45 when he was addressing Nathanael. There are two things in play here. The assertion that Philip found Jesus and the fact that Jesus called Philip are in play. As stated above, whether one finds Jesus and gives his life or whether Jesus finds the person, the choice of God is the determinative one as MacArthur (2003, p. 123) writes basing his notion on John 15: 16:

> "You did not choose me, but I chose you and appointed you so that you might go and bear fruit— fruit that will last—and so that whatever you ask in my name the Father will give you."

Philip's view that he said, "We have found the Messiah," also states that Philip was looking for the Messiah to come. He had a heart overly waiting for the Messiah. It shows a prepared heart, unhesitating and gladly accepting heart (MacArthur 2003, p. 124).

It shows a believing heart that depended on the word of God and finally assured that the word was true as Philip found the anticipated Messiah.

According to MacArthur (2003, p. 124) Philip's heart was an expectant heart, it was a heart of no unbelief, it was the heart different from Nathanael. The heart of Nathanael was a questioning heart although the questioning was from a genuine understanding. Nathanael's heart was obsessed with the importance of a place-as he said does something good come out of Nazareth. Philip's heart was obsessed with the importance of the person of the Messiah. A place is not important but the Messiah was, proofing the truth that Philip was dragged to a man from Nazareth assuring that all that the Father gives comes to Christ (John 6:37).

In conclusion, according to MacArthur (2003, p. 124), Philip had unhesitant heart to follow Christ. This asserts that Philip was in complete dependency on Christ. Philip was not unsure of his future. He believed that his future was guaranteed and secured. Assured of the future, Philip abandoned his belongings including his fishing profession and followed Christ.

A description of Philip

Evangelism: was not an open air evangelist. He was someone who hunts individuals for Christ. Accordingly, upon his conversion to be the student of Christ, he brought his best friend Nathanael to Christ. He knew that no one is more important in the life of Nathanael than Jesus Christ. Thus, he brought Nathanael to the Messiah.

Philip knew that Jesus is without choice necessary for people. Philip also knew that he is not called to be idle. Philip exhibited that his call was to reach to others and tell about Christ. Believing in Christ, to be the student of Christ pushes one from a comfort zone to tell others about Jesus and this telling starts from a backyard, from our best friends- the many Nathanaels that we have. As he reached for Nathanael and let him surrender to Christ, Philip disclosed what the call to be the student/matheetees/μαθητής is meant about.

To be the student/matheetees/μαθητής of Christ is a commission to reach to the lost world and that reaching starts from our nearest environments. There are so many unreached individuals in our surroundings. A true student/matheetees/μαθητής is one who is ready to reach to his/her environment. A true student/ matheetees/ μαθητής focuses on the souls without Christ in his neighborhood and Philip's call bore that fruit immediately he was found and made the student of Christ.

Food Distribution and Supplies: According to MacArthur (2003, p. 125) Philip was seen as a person in charge of administering meals and logistics. Glenn Cummings (2008, p. 42) writes that Philip was the apostolic administrator which MacArthur (2003, p. 125) states as "the bean counter." This is avowed from the question that Jesus projected out in handpicking Philip when He was to feed the hungry crowds in John 6. None of the other disciples were addressed with this question and it was for a reason that Philip was asked. In fact, John 6: 5 states that Jesus was to test Philip. Jesus was to test Philip because He knew that Philip was a professional meal and logistics administrator. Cummings (p. 42) notes that Philip was a man concerned in organization and administration.

Given his skills in meal admiration and organization, Philip had the experience of how to feed many people but not as many as 5000 men (MacArthur, 2003, p. 125). Philip had the experience of how to handle great multitudes and in fact Jesus' testing question was to see how Philip reacts amidst the shortage of food supplies and the demand for food was too much as there were many crowds waiting for food.

The shortage of supplies is not in terms of Jesus' divine power; it is only in terms of human understanding because no mathematics or logic proves those five loaves of bread and two fishes (John 6: 9) feed five thousand men. Five thousand men is with the exclusion of the number of women and children. If Children and women were counted, the crowds could be about 15,000 to 20, 000 (Cummings, 2008, p.42). It is simply a denial of truth if one argues that this amount of available food is enough for this number of people. But the eyes of faith are beyond the existence of material substance. The eyes of faith are beyond the availability of food supplies. They see miracles, the coming of manna and the finest flour flourishing amidst famine (2Kings 7: 1). They stick to the heart of faith than the mind of Math. In the mind of Math an insignificant amount of food cannot be multiplied to feed as many as 20,000 individuals and the left over is collected. It is only in the mind and heart of faith that an insignificant is multiplied to feed millions.

A Student who failed his Exam; Philip: Philip was not only a student but also a professional food administrator who handles complex issues in relation to feeding people (Cummings (2008, 42). No one knows from where he got this experience. But without experience, as one infers from John 6: 5 Jesus could not bring Philip into a test. Philip was brought to a test here in John 6 not as a student in a normal class room but as an experienced administrator. Jesus handpicked Philip for a test knowing what Jesus himself will be doing. Philip, unlike his profession, failed the test. Philip depended on the mind of Math and calculation. As put to the test, Philip began his Mathematical proof saying as in John 6: 7 "It would take more than half a year's wages to buy enough bread for each one to have a bite!" This answer of Philip asserts that, "It is impossible," Cummings (2008, 43).

According to Cummings (2008, p. 43) "the impossible does not take Jesus extra time at all." "He specializes in the impossible." No one knows how Philip lost the mind and heart of the Lord of the impossible. Philip has been in the miracle laboratories of Jesus since his call. Philip like any other disciples saw Jesus healing the impossible. He saw Jesus changing water into wine, and Jesus reading the very heart of the apostle Nathanael whom Philip himself brought to Jesus. Philip knew that Jesus as the bread of life and the Lord of the impossible was at his side when put to the test. But Philip failed. Philip failed big (Cummings, 2008, p. 42). Philip could have returned the test question into his Lord and said my Math does not work so I surrender everything to you. According to Cummings (2008, p. 43) Philip, "could have put aside his materialistic, pragmatic, common sense solutions and lay hold of the supernatural power that comes from the Living Lord," Because Philip stick to the earthly brain, the knowledge of reason and logic, he failed and he failed miserably.

A Student who missed his reference book: The Greeks wanted to be introduced to Jesus in John 12: 20-22. Perhaps the reason the Greeks came to Philip was that he was the apostle with a Greek name and they thought that he was Greek in origin or may be speaking Greek. Also, it is argued that the Greeks who came to Philip were from the same town Philip grew up. They might possess the same culture and linguistic make up. Also, the Greeks had information that Philip was the administrator who makes arrangements and in charge of the operations on behalf of the disciples according to MacArthur (2003, 128).

The reason why Philip sought the help of Andrew to introduce these Greeks to Jesus was yet unknown. It can be argued that Philip consulted Andrew if it was proper to move the Greeks request to Christ. The notion that arises from here is why Philip as a student of Christ needs the consultation of Andrew when he had full access to Christ. Why he did not do by himself? According to Click (2000, p. 28) Philip was not willing to take responsibility. He wants to put the responsibility as a shared with Andrew. This may be because the Greeks were gentiles and Jesus had already told them not to go the gentiles' territory (Matthew 10:5). Jesus also addressed that he was sent to the lost sheep of Israel (Matthew 15: 24). Due to this, Philip was afraid to take the responsibility of taking gentiles to the Lord by himself. `But this principle which prohibits the gentiles from accessing Christ was simply a normal priority in ministry according to MacArthur (2003, p. 124) which was written in Romans 2:10; to

Jew first and also to the Greeks. Then, why did Philip afraid to take the Greeks to Christ?

Philip is a person rigid to rules (MacArthur 2003, p. 124). He was a person committed to the inviolability of rules (P. 124). Because of this, he thought that taking the Greeks to Christ was in violation of the set rules. Also, Philip did not perfectly understood Jesus' ministry priority. Philip missed the notion of "priority," reaching to the Jews first as the assertion that Jesus was limited to the Jews (p. 124).

The Jesus to whom Philip was called to be a student was beyond certain cultural and linguistic groups. Jesus was the God of the global environment to whom every race from every corner is welcomed. Jesus himself said in John 6:37 that "All those the Father gives me will come to me, and whoever comes to me I will never drive away." Also, Jesus ministered to the gentiles in the very eyes of the disciples. He reached to the Samaritans. It was absurd that Philip missed his reference book. Philip could gladly welcome the Samaritans by himself and connected the Greeks to Christ. Philip had full access to Christ to bring anyone to Jesus. At this point, it is asserted that Philip lost his reference book. Jesus was Philip's lost central reference book and anyone was to be referred to Jesus.

A Student who missed the Lord: Despite his years of experience as an administrator and business operation, Philip did not known who Jesus was. Jesus was teaching, healing, miraculously feeding thousands, walking on water, telling His disciples that He was the light of the world, the bread of life, the living water, the good shepherd, the gate but even to the last hours Philip did not get Jesus. At a time when Jesus was to be handed over to be crucified, He comforted His disciples in the upper room. He administered the last supper, washed their feet, promised the coming of the Holy Spirit. Jesus also promised that He was going to prepare a place for them. Jesus farther promised that He will be back to receive them to Himself (John 14: 3-7). As He goes, Jesus said He is the way to the

Father. He alone is the savior and the way and only way to the Father. As Jesus was speaking this, He also explicitly claimed deity and said in John 14:7: "If you really know me, you will know my Father as well. From now on, you do know him and have seen him."

Jesus clearly expressed that He was God and He and His Father are the same. Thus, anyone who saw Jesus has seen God as the persons of the Trinity are one in essence. Although Jesus spoke His Lordship in the clearest terms and that He is God, Philip immediately missed the point. John14: 8: Philip said, "Lord, show us the Father and that will be enough for us."

Philip did not know that Jesus is God even when Jesus was speaking to him. According to MacArthur (2003, 133) Philip was imperfect, a person with limited understanding like the other disciples, a man of weak faith. Philip was unsure, reluctant and a student who depended on figures and facts (P. 133). Above all, it is sad to see Philip miserably failed. Philip was with the living and eternal God (p. 132). He did not need any more miracle and any more proof (p. 132). He was in the face of this God for three years (p. 133) but did not know yet. Philip was still looking for a better proof, a better miracle and a more profound evidence to see God the Father but God the Father was right there with him. He is the Lord that called him from the village of Bethsaida while he was fishing. But why was Philips's mind so small to recognize Jesus? MacArthur (p. 133) writes,

> His earthbound thinking, his materialism, his skepticism, his obsession with mundane details, his preoccupation with business details, and his small mindedness had shut him off a full apprehension of whose presence he had enjoyed.

It is asserted now that Philip had missed the Lord and he failed in the strongest terms. He was a student who was looking for the more when even the more he was looking for was with him. He missed the mark. You cannot find what you have unless you missed it. But Philip missed on his shelf. He could not see what is available or what he saw was not what he was looking for. He was demanding more and unsatisfied although he saw and Jesus was telling him that He was God and performing things that a divine power could do. Jesus responded to Philip's questions of seeking to see God as follows in John 14: 9–11:

> Jesus answered: "Don't you know me, Philip, even after I have been among you such a long time? Anyone who has seen me has seen the Father. How can you say, 'Show us the Father'? Don't you believe that I am in the Father, and that the Father is in me? The words I say to you I do not speak on my own authority. Rather, it is the Father, living in me, who is doing his work. Believe me when I say that I am in the Father and the Father is in me; or at least believe on the evidence of the works themselves.

Conclusion: Philip was looking for more proof; he was demanding, unsatisfied, a person of logic, reason and could not enjoy the full apprehensions of God. Convincing facts, provable things are those that change Philip. The best example to this is how he reacted when Jesus asked him about the hungry crowds in John 6. Philip's answers were dependent on tangible facts, mathematical operations than the power of Christ. He was trying to convince Christ that there is nothing that satisfies the hungry crowds. Philip stated that what is available is a complete scarce and does not feed these numbers of crowds. Philip was not in a position to depend on Jesus. He did not recognize that Jesus was the God of miracle who multiples the insignificant, the scarce into a huge banquet. He did not recognize that Jesus possessed the power to feed the hungry by multiplying our meager resources. Why was then Philip included among the twelve?

Jesus was always looking for those people who were not able to see beyond immediate circumstances, slow to trust Him and demanding.

These were the features of Philip according to MacArthur (2003, p. 133). MacArthur (p. 133) also writes that Jesus was exactly looking for such individuals as Jesus' strength is made perfect in weaknesses. Yes, Philip had many weaknesses and his weakness could have resulted in his expulsion from the teams of Christ's students from human point of view but Jesus has never been looking for those who were strong. Jesus was calling people who had human tendencies that hamper their faith. Philip possessed such human tendencies throughout his walk with Christ and he failed in many ways but that was the power of Christ where the weak, the foolish looking are called for eternal destiny. Despite the many shortcomings, Philip was proved to be one of the apostles that planted churches, completed the Great Commission and stoned to death for his faith in Asian minor bringing multitudes to Christ (p. 133).

11. James Son of Alphas

According to Click (2000, p.44) James the son of Alphas was the least know of the apostles. MacArthur (2003, p. 170-171) supports this stating that James the son of Alphas was utterly obscured and the only thing scripture holds about this man is his name. The scripture also notes that he was the son of Alphaeus (Mark 10:3; Mark 3: 18; Luke 6: 15; Acts 1:13.) Besides this, the scripture notes that his mother's name was Mary (Mark 15; 47). Over all, James's history is scanty and what is available is his parents' name. Also, MacArthur (p. 171) mentions that Mary was the woman who came to prepare Jesus' body for burial (Mark 16:1). One infers from this that James grew up in a committed family of Christ. That probably shaped his life and ministry. Yet, still the history of this apostle is completely obscured and Click (2000, p. 44) observes that James was "the patron saint of the nameless."

James, like many of the other students of Christ had a nick name. In Mark 15: 40 he was named "James the Less," according to MacArthur (2003, p. 171). The name "Less," is "micros" in Greek which means "little," in the words of MacArthur (p.171). James' nick name depicts two things. First, it shows a physical appearance which means he was probably short (P. 171). Second, it means he was young. That means he was probably younger than James the son of Zebedee and it was used to distinguish him from Zebedee's son (P. 171). That means he may not be the youngest of all as the youngest among them was thought to be Judas the son of James. The nick name also depicts that James the son of Alphaeus was not participating in many things and he may be depicted as "small," as he was in a backyard in obscurity (P. 172). His participation among the students of Christ was absent from recorded history but James was included among the twelve for a reason.

Conclsuion: Although scanty records are available about James, he contributed a lot in the expansion of the kingdom of God and Click (2000, p. 44) states that he preached in Syria and Russia before his martyrdom. MacArthur (2003, 173) writes that James preached in Persia and stoned to death, or beaten or died or crucified like His Lord.

An interesting thing is that James was the brother of Matthew (Mark 2: 14), one of the apostles. Matthew was the son of Alphaeus and James too but the scripture does not clearly state that they were brothers (MacArthur, p.173). Since he went quietly unnoticed in the Gospel narratives (P. 173), the world does not remember much of him but he will be receiving rewards in heaven (Mark 10: 29-31) according to MacArthur (p. 173).

12. Judas Iscariot

Name and Birth Place

The New Testament does not reveal much about Judas' family and the environment he grew up (George E. Meisinger, 2004). It is surmised from his surname "Iscariot" that he probably was a man from Karioth. There are theories surrounding the meaning of Karioth. One of the theories attests that the name refers to a town. This theory is used by Meisinger (2004) who asserts that Iscariot refers to a man from Karioth. In this case, Karioth refers to a place which scholars assume as a place in Southern Judea (Meisinger, 2004). MacArthur (2003, p. 182) supports this notion stating that Iscariot is the name of a region where Iscariot is derived from the Hebrew words "Ish" and Karioth. "Ish" means man and Karioth means town meaning a man from Karioth. Karioth in modern history may be Kerioth, which is a small town in Judea about 15 miles from South of Hebron (Meisinger, 2 004). Judas Iscariot was the only Judean among the twelve students/ disciples of Christ.

Call

According to Anthony Cane (2017, p. 15) the first mention of Judas Iscariot in the Synoptic gospels occur in relation to Jesus' nomination of "the twelve." Cane (p.15) writes that the list of the twelve begins with Peter at the head and Judas at the last. Cane (p. 15) also states that the call came from Christ and Christ alone asserting that the call of Judas was not humanly. Mark 13: 13–14 depicts as follows:

> Everyone will hate you because of me, but the one who stands firm to the end will be saved. "When you see 'the abomination that causes desolation' standing where it does not belong—let the reader understand—then let those who are in Judea flee to the mountains.

Cane (2017, p. 15) also explains that Jesus makes the twelve. That means it was not Judas who made himself the student/disciple of Christ. To be a student/disciple of Christ is a matter of making and that making only comes from heaven making the calling of Judas a total divine plan but that does not mean to be a disciple is to be perfect. Vincent Taylor quoted in Cane (p. 15-16) writes that studentship/discipleship did not mean immediate perfection but left open the hard road of temptation. As stated repeatedly Jesus did not call unfailing disciples but un-quitting. This notion asserts that through not quitting disciples grow into perfection. Judas Iscariot missed this opportunity of growth only by self-choice driven by a passion for greed, lies and unfaithfulness. MacArthur (2003, p.197) writes that "Judas was a waste of privilege whose highest place of privilege-cashed for a fistful of coins," the coins that he did not use because of a guilt that he did not seek forgiveness for.

A description of Judas

The Power of Money: Unlike the other disciples, Judas' call was not recorded in the scripture (MacArthur 2003, 183). But one may accurately describe that he was called by Jesus to be a life time student. A life time student demands a matter of not quitting. It does not matter if one fails as the call of the students/ disciples of Christ is not defined by failures. The entire team failed in the course of their walk with Christ but eleven students committed to the end without quitting but entertaining multiple failures in life.

Judas was not among the not quitting, he was succumbed into the roots of all evil- the love of money. That love of all evil consumed him from inside out snatching him by his own choice from the hands of the Lord. MacArthur (p. 197) defined Judas as follows:

> Judas was the epitome of wasted privilege. He was given the highest place of privilege-cashed it in for a fistful of coins he decided he did not really want it at all…!

This summary of who Judas details the notion that even lest looking- a fist of coins- would bring devastating impact on a person that does not care about his/her call (MacArthur, 2000, p. 197). The call of Jesus is something above any other thing. It is not something we sell for not only less important but also the precious things of this world.

Judas was in a materialistic mindset and was greedily looking for it. According to Tom Houston (1986, p. 23) there are many theories and guesses about Judas Iscariot ranging from disillusioned zealot to be a nationalist. More than this, according to Houston (P. 23) the New Testament treated Judas accurately as someone trapped in the love of money leading into his betrayal of Jesus Christ.

One cannot betray Jesus for money only but money and money only defined Judas as he was the bank of the twelve carrying the money bag and stealing from it as narrated in John 12: 6:

> He did not say this because he cared about the poor
> but because he was a thief; as keeper of the money
> bag, he used to help himself to what was put into it.

No one knows what type of accounting talent Judas had to create a financial conspiracy that assisted him to steal from the collections of Jesus' squad. It is not warranted that having an accounting talent leads to financial cheating or stealing but in the case of Judas one can accurately describe him of money stealing through some sort of accounting talent he grasped in his lifetime.

Judas was all about stealing, someone filled with attack on those who were doing good for Jesus as in his furious but systemic love painted towards the needy when Mary brought the expensive perfume to Jesus (John 12: 4). It was cosmetically painted love because superficially, it looked like a help towards the needy but deep inside it was a materialistic nature of Judas where his heart was lying on stealing money out of the sale of the perfume had the perfume been sold and the money was put in the "common purse".

Money has the power where people in charge of money like Judas can do whatever they want, succumbing to money's lasting effect on human life. According to Eduard Porter (2013) in the NY Times, the power of money is described as follows:

> From Judas Iscariot, who betrayed Jesus for 30 pieces
> of silver … human history is full of examples of

money's ability to weaken even the firmest ethical backbone." "Money sows mistrust. It ends friendships. Experiments have found that it encourages us to lie and cheat. As Karl Marx, the scourge of capitalism, noted, "Money then appears as the enemy of man and social bonds that pretend to self-subsistence.

Liar: According to Cane (2017, p. 17) the meaning of "Iscariot indicates that Judas was from Kerioth, or was a bandit to that it was a nickname meaning liar or false one." This was one of the theories behind the meaning of Iscariot but a theory that accurately describes who Judas was given his characters among the twelve which the Bible describes as thief (John 12: 6). To lie is an action and Iscariot is a name where the actions of Judas depict his identification. Liddell and Scott quoted in Cane (p. 19-20) take note of Mark 3: 19 and explain that Judas Iscariot, based on his actions written in Mark 3: 19 which in Greek is παρέδωκεν meaning "give up to the enemy, betray, paly false, prove traitor or to be false" to elaborate that Judas Iscariot was a liar. But this notion creates a question if one can becomes both a liar and a thief simultaneously.

Is to be a liar makes someone a thief or is to be a thief makes someone a liar? Judas was described as a thief in the Bible which means he was stealing and identified as a liar based on the Greek word παρέδωκεν which means false one or liar according to Liddell and Scott quoted in Cane (p. 19-20).

The two words, "Lying and stealing" are actions and they are overlapping only if they are based on "intent." Intended lying and stealing are not honest mistakes and accidents. They are committed on purpose and intently (Jennifer Bloomquist 2010, p. 1597). Bloomquist (p. 1604) writes that stealing and lying have relationships to one another. According to this, one who steals lies and one who lies steals. In fact, there is an overlap of lying and stealing concepts with fraud which incorporates elements from each: lying and cheating in order to steal (p. 1604). In this case, Judas was stealing from the "common fund" with the intention that his stealing was also involving lying to the group, probably in reporting. Judas' actions were thus both lying and stealing, giving him the name of a thief and a liar. One cannot be a liar or a thief without the other. Both actions go together especially in financial fraud identifying Judas as a thief and a liar. Also, both actions stealing and lying depict that Judas was unfaithful. Furthermore, to be a liar is an identity; it explains who someone is. To be a thief is also an identity. Both a "liar and a thief" were names given to the devil in the Bible not as an action but as identities where the identities take to the actions. Does that mean Judas was a devil?

The devil was identified as a liar in the gospel of John (John 8:44) and the same identification was given to Judas which means Judas was not only a liar based on his actions but also based on his identity. The devil gets into Judas in John 13: 27 and Luke 22: 3. According to John 13: 27 the devil possessed Judas. That means Judas was controlled. Judas did not have freedom of himself other than serving his mater; the devil. That service is not as an identity but as an action. Yet it can be argued that Judas was transformed into a newborn where that new born depicts an identity. The new birth here is similar to a believer's new birth in Christ to be a child of Christ. Similarly, Judas was newly born as a child of the devil; taking the actual identity of the devil as a liar and a thief. That means Judas became the devil in a complete shift of life from the child of Christ to the devil abandoning his studentship status in Christ. This change of identity finally crushed Judas to death as the power of the devil and the power of Christ were antagonistic and should not stand together.

By all account, Judas Iscariot's devilish identity was doing everything belonging to the world and against the kingdom of God. From greed to lies and from trying to commodify the Master Jesus as an object and thus diminishing the value of Christ into a fist of coins, Judas was filled with works of the devil not only doing it as an action but also as an identity. That finally led Judas to be trapped by his actions leading him to suicide and unforgivable offence. Judas Iscariot was called to be a student of Christ to the end growing into the likeness of Christ, but by his own choices and by his own identity, he failed and without regret succumbed to death wasting his years of time with Christ.

Conclusion: Judas life was simply an outward show with no conversion from the inside. It was an outward loyalty with no following from the heart. He even had no heart to seek forgiveness and finally committed suicide. He was a lost opportunity by his own choice. Although chosen for the divine mission as a student in the studentship process, his life continued to be wastage. If one learns anything from Judas Iscariot, it will be the notion that any minor thing; a fist of coin ruins our life. This presses that our walk as a student with Christ, needs care, attachment, commitment and prioritizing Christ. Judas Iscariot did not prioritize Christ over lies, coins, and greed.

What does the call to be a disciple involve?

1. It involves growth process

The call to be a disciple does not mean the process is complete and dead ones a person is a disciple. It is like an infant growing into a toddler and a young adult into adulthood. It is a process and it leads into maturity where the maturity is to the fullness of Christ. Quoting Lawrence Richards, Greg Ogden (2016, p. 96) summarizes this as follows:

> The Christian life is described in various New Testament passages as growth from spiritual infancy to maturity. The new believer starts as an infant and eventually grows up in Christ. One moves from the state of dependency, in which others model, teach, and disciple, to a mature walk with God. As this growth occurs, the believer also begins to assume

disciplining responsibility for others. While it is true that the believer is always dependent on God and the Holy Spirit in that growth process, there is a natural progression in maturity which leads the believer to be used by God to serve and minister to others.

Ogden farther asserts quoting Bailiwicks (p. 96) that to be a student of Christ is similar to parenting which empowers children to maturity. This leads the children to gain power and finally make decisions of their own and go beyond their primary Island. Similarly, after successfully parented disciples go beyond their boundaries and reach out to others as the sign of their growth.

This level of growth starts at home where home is a church for a disciple and parents' homes for children (Ogden, p.197). These are primary units where disciplining and parenting starts. This growing process goes to the complete maturity in Christ. This maturity is "telos" in Greek and it means "end" or "goal" (p. 98). "To be mature means to be fully adult," (p. 98) which is impossible without instructions where those instructed fully reach the level of maturity as opposed to novices or those in Catechumens (p. 98). The students of Christ are called into maturity- into full adult hood but it is also a choice to remain in infancy where the infancy is to remain in catechumens or novices.

The greatest problem that one observes in a global church is that students are either not instructed to reach adulthood or chosen to remain in infancy. Every believer is called into discipleship- into a studentship of Christ- to be a disciple and in the process of discipleship which are simultaneous occurrences in the believer's life and these occurrences need parenting to reach to the level of "telos" (Ogden, 2016, p. 82).

"Telos" demands a continuous process of uninterrupted instructions. Jesus is always in the continuous process of giving instructions to any student in His school. He noted that He is the teacher and the student is called to learn and this learning involves growing into maturity as Paul explicated to the Corinthian church that they could have been adults when they were still infants in their spiritual nutrition (1 Corinthians 3: 1-4). This notion asserts that to be an infant in Christ is unwelcome but to be the infant of Christ is. An infant grows into adulthood and one of the call of Christ's students was to reach that level.

According to Ogden (p. 79) the students of Christ were growing from mere observant or examiners to apostles where Jesus delegated them with full confidence that they would complete the assignment entrusted to them in the presence of the un-orphaning father. It is clear that a process of growth is in display here. An observer cannot be an examiner and an apostle automatically. To be an observer, then an examiner and then an apostle is a process where the process involves growth. Jesus called growing children. The children of Christ are always growing and uninterruptedly. Their growth is a continuous process.

2. Lifetime Commitment

The disciple of Christ was a student but very different from a student attending lessons in the classroom from a teacher. This student is different in reality that he/she displays lifetime commitment to the end and to the extreme. To the end here refers to the end of a temporary walk of life in this world blameless and in continual connection to Christ. To the extreme on the other hand elucidates the notion of carrying one's cross. A cross is life difficulties, challenges, temptations and obstacles in a student's walk of life with Christ. Jesus taught that anyone who follows him carries his/her own cross not the cross of Christ as in Luke 14. 26. A student here also differs from a student in a normal class in a way that this student has Christ in his/her life. Christ is more than a teacher in this sense that it involves not only the over lordship of Christ as a Master in one's life but also an unbroken relationship where the student has Christ in his/her life and Christ has him/her.

3. In a Commitment and not in a commitment

The commitment part is a commitment of walking to the end with Christ passing victoriously any life difficulties that may tempt our faith. A life that is not demanding commitment on the other hand is that a student in this school is not called to carry the cross of its Master. The cross of the Master is once and for all completed on the cross of Christ and none is called to carry that cross or none is called to that commitment, but that cross enables any student in this school to carry his/her cross. Thus, a student here is both called to a commitment and not a commitment. In addition, while the cross of Christ is one and only one and un-repetitive, the crosses of a student are diverse and repetitive, challenging the students' walk for the growth into the likeness of Christ. This asserts that the cross of Christ is committed to the student as the student is committed to carrying his/her cross. This notion concludes that a commitment to Christ without the cross of Christ is impossible.

A disciple/a student commits him/herself not to carry the cross of Christ which is central in the believer's life but because one is called to be a follower he/she carries his/her own cross. This cross that a disciple carries is not a burden as the cross of Christ to which we are not committed nor called to carry enables us in our walk with Christ. Contrasting this notion, Luther elucidates that the cross on Golgotha is the one a follower carries all his/her life and there is no dichotomy between a disciple's cross and the Cross of Christ. Grannis, Laffin, &Schade (1981, p. 16) assert this notion detailing that disciples are called to carry the cross of Christ. Simpson (2015, p. 12) avows this as the identification of a believer with Christ and writes as follows:

The tests of the Master must be applied to His followers. We may not preach a crucified Savior without also being crucified men and women. It is not enough to wear an ornamental cross as a pretty decoration. The cross that Paul speaks about was burned into his very flesh, was branded into his being; and only the Holy Ghost can burn the true cross into our innermost life. We are saved by identification with Christ in His death. We are justified because we have already died with Him and have thus been made free from sin. God does not whitewash people when He saves them. He has really visited their sins upon their great Substitute, the Lord Jesus Christ, and every believer was counted as in Him when He died; and so His death is our death and it puts us in the same position before the law of the supreme Judge as if we had already been executed and punished for our own guilty, as if the judgment for us was already past. Therefore, it is true of every believer, ""Very truly I tell you, whoever hears my word and believes him who sent me has eternal life and will not be judged but has crossed over from death to life." (John 5:24). The cross, therefore, is the very standpoint of the believer's salvation, and we shall never cease to echo the song of heaven.

But this understanding is disputed on the fact that the Cross of Christ is the one that took Christ to death for the salvation of all. It was the cross in the past with the present effect. The present effect avows the truth that the churches preaching, and teaching is null without it as it is the singular source for salvation. Contrasting this is the cross of a believer that neither saves the believer nor anyone. Although it has no saving power, it can be asserted that a believer's cross cannot exist without the Master's cross. We are identified with Christ and part of the identification is to be marked with the cross of Christ. Dietrich Bonhoeffer (1959, p.79) asserts this, "a believer's cross is laid on him."

In general, one observes that there are two crosses in the believers' life. The cross of Christ and the cross of a believer where the believer's cross is invalid without the cross of Christ. The cross of a believer is in fact laid on a believer as a bid to come and die (Bonhoeffer 1959, p. 79). The word "laid" references here that the cross of a believer is put by somebody else depicting that the cross itself was something the believer takes from Christ. This cross of a believer "brings real suffering," but "God is there, offering us something far greater – the promise of life in all its fullness." According to Danny Lim (2017) the cross of a believer is generated from the cross of Christ asserting that without the cross of Christ the believer's cross is nothing. While the cross of Christ is saving the individual, the cross that a believer carries has no power of saving except taking the believer into the likeness of Christ in services.

4. Called to a school with or without certificate

A student in this school has no certificate in his/her lifetime. Unlike the worldly schools that confer certificates, degrees and other credentials at some point in the life of a student, there is no certificate in the school of Christ at a certain age. There is no paper certificate that a follower displays. The only certificate available to a follower is Jesus Himself. The only certificate is the person of Christ. The only certificate is salvation through the person of Christ that a student totally embraces at the end of the worldly life or during the second coming of Christ in the kingdom.

Paul writes that we are sealed in Ephesians 1:13. Paul also writes that we bear the marks of Christ in Galatians (Galatians 6: 17). How can one be sealed without any certification? How can one carry the marks of Christ without certificate? Marks and Seals are things that are displayed outside and can be seen. They are things put on a certificate, a degree paper, and a graduation paper of a certain individual from the higher authority as a symbol of completion. It carries with it responsibilities and accountabilities for the individual upon whom the degree is conferred. If marks and seals are displayed, they cannot be hidden. How about in the school of Christ?

In the school of Christ if the Apostle Paul is a guide to us as in Galatians 6: 17, it avows that the marks of a believer are brands-brands of Christ which means a believer is distinguished with this brand. This distinguishing brand is a unique mark of Christ. It means the believer is submitted to his/her Master in obedience. This mark/seal is a mark that comes through service, suffering for Christ and is also a security. It is a security for salvation and a security that guards against unfaithfulness amidst dangers. Since it guards against dangers, since it is a security and since it is something that distinguishes a believer, it is something seen from a believer.

5. It involves Obedience

No discipleship begins without obedience. Studentship in Christ demands absolute obedience and sacrifice (Garland, 1996, p. 84). According to Dietrich Bonhoeffer (1959, p. 48) a call and the obedience of the disciples into the school of Christ was an absolute, direct and unaccountable authority of Christ. Michael J. Wilkins (2004, p. 187) asserts this stating that obedience is the only appropriate answer to Jesus' authoritative call. Wilkins (p. 187) states that "when Jesus calls to whatever, we must immediately obey." The "only appropriate answer" and "the must to obey" (Wilkins, p 187) the call clears that both the Call and the obedience are divine and inseparable. Bonhoeffer (p. 48) asserts that Jesus has the authority to call and to demand obedience neither as a teacher nor as a pattern of the good life but as the Christ, the Son of God which squarely puts the notion that both the call and the obedience were divine. But it has to be warranted that obedience to the call was also the complete decision of the disciples. Both the disciples' decision to follow the call and the authority of Christ were compatible.

Obedience and the call into the discipleship as a student is an exit in its strict sense where the disciple forsakes his/her old life burning his/her boat from the life of relative security into the life of insecurities but in truth into the security and safety of the fellowship of Jesus Christ (Bonhoeffer, 1959, p. 49). Choosing insecurity other than security is a matter of divine call and complete obedience into the supreme call of Christ. Obedience to the unknown future forsaking the present safety demands obedience but it is a call into an exclusive attachment of the person of Christ (P. 49). To be a student in the school of Christ does not depend on the situations that force someone into obedience, it does not look into the brightness of the future nor the darkness of the present or yesterday, but it is attached to the person of Christ.

6. It involves Choice and Obedience

You are the result of your choice. In her book the Power of Onlyness, Nilofer Merchant (2017, p. 6) argued that choices define each of us. It means that we are products of our choices. In fact, people are the product of their choices in academics, in politics, in economics, clothing, vehicle brands, etc. These choices shape, define and decide who we are and our futures. This understanding asserts that we are made who we are because of the choices we made in life regardless that they are bad or good. We are not the products of fortunes, but we are either the products of our careless or thoughtful choices. We are not even the result of our abilities according to J.K. Rowling, Harry Potter and the Chamber of Secrets (J.K.Rowling, 1998). Merchant (2017, p. 6) noted without questioning one's ability that choices define our path, open up doors of opportunities for our purposes.

Despite Merchant's understanding, we are also the result of both our choices and other people's choices. The disciples of Christ choose their discipleship path only because the Master chose them, but that choice was complete because the disciples were obedient to it. Although the choice was prompted from their Master, it was complete because of the obedience generated from the disciples themselves. Jesus as the choice generator, was the one in whom they were defined. The choice explained them, directed their destiny and willingly called them to leave everything and follow Christ. The choice was a book showing them their direction where they were heading and their ultimate end. The entire lives of the disciples were explained and defined in this choice, a choice that came not from them but from their Master. This nullifies Nilofer Merchant's (2017, p. 6) thought that we are the result of our choices. Yes, we are but we, as believers are the choices of our Master; Jesus Christ.

According to Greg Ogden (2016, p. 79) the call to follow Jesus was demanding a yes or no answer. A yes shows that the called disciple is willing where the no is a reversal. In fact, divine choice, as Jesus said in John 15: 16, "I have chosen you" was ultimate mark of discipleship in the discipleship school of taught but that was complete because of the willingness, commitment and choosing the chooser of the disciples. You are chosen but the chooser's choose is complete only if the chosen is obedient to the chooser saying "yes" to follow. The chooser is thus unsuccessful unless the chosen abides to the call. In fact, as elucidated, the chooser, Jesus Christ is the one who brings the called into obedience, but obedience is complete when the one called accepts the call in obedience. The disciples as they accepted their call through obedience asserted saying in Matthew 19: 27, "we have left everything and followed you." The call and the commitment to following through obedience was the disciples choose yet Jesus command into obedience.

A choice determines your future. In one way or another we live our choices. Our choice to obedience in the school of Christ comes into complete as a call into the kingdom of God was effected in Christ. Both the disciples' ultimate choice of obedience and the call into discipleship were instant and simultaneous.

7. It involves a journey

A journey is a trip or a voyage to a certain place with a specific destination or an unknown place. A journey of a disciple is a journey to the unknown as it was an instant call with no knowledge of where to go but accompanied with obedience. It was even an unknown trip because it was sudden, instant response to a call from a Galilean man Jesus Christ whose knowledge was at most bare in the minds of the disciples. Ogden (p. 63) disputes this elucidating that the disciples had prior connection with Christ as Jesus called them into investigative instruction in John where He said come and see(John 1: 39). Affirming this, Greg Ogden (2003, p. 64) writes that the disciples were seekers and later came to a decision after they authenticated the identity of the engaging person; Jesus Christ. This idea states that the disciples' decision to be the true students of Christ came at a later time although the specificity of the later time is not known. It shows that the disciples' growth into the final decision to be true students of Christ was a process than an instant immediate decision.

Discipleship is a lifelong process. It is a lifetime journey, a journey that begins immediately upon admission to the school of Christ. This admission is a call and not a personal achievement. This call is instant that also makes being a disciple an instant happening in the life of a disciple or a student of Christ. To be a student of Christ or a disciple is not a process but discipleship involves a process. David Garland (1996, p. 79-80) quoting Lohmeyer writes that Jesus commands as God commands. This command is the command that creates things from nothing. It is the command that brings unimaginable things into existence. This power according to Garland (p. 79) propels the disciples to follow Christ. It does not simply propel them to follow, it also makes them disciples. This effectively contrasts Ogden's understanding (Ogden, 2003, p. 64) of a later time decision into discipleship of the disciples' of Christ. While discipleship and being a disciple begin automatically in the life of a disciple or a student of Christ, discipleship is a process where the disciple grows. To grow one has to be planted first. Once planted in Christ, the disciple begins a growth process- which is discipleship or studentship. Analogically, in a secular classroom, a student upon admission cannot be an engineer nor a medical doctor nor a psychologist nor a theologian but remains a student with a process to become a professional in a specific field. While there is a set time for a student in a secular schooling system to become a professional engineer, medical doctor, etc., there is no set time for a student/disciple of Christ to complete discipleship process but each day counts to become like Christ. This process is a journey of faith where the student/ disciple is required to walk. It is a lifetime trip.

It is a trip with Jesus, a journey accompanied and a journey undetached from the person of Jesus Christ. It was a journey with a beginning and an end as the complete geography of where a disciple goes is the person of Christ. This journey is a lifelong journey of faith. It is not a marathon race, nor a journey began today and ends tomorrow. It is a matter of a lifetime commitment. It is a journey with and in complete "adherence to Christ, because Christ is the object of that adherence" as avowed by Bonhoeffer (1959, p. 50).

8. It involves a New direction/ a different walk

The disciples of Christ have been living the life that any ordinary Galilean has been living. They were working and have been in routine day to day activity in Galilee. They had their own personal plan and day to day job description. In a sudden move someone they did not see in their lifetime came up and shattered everything that they own. He shattered their plan. He took their opportunities. He gave them a different map other than the map they already knew; the Galilean topography. He gave them a different direction than the old life direction that they knew.

The life experience they knew was just going to their daily routine activities. Their experience was just working and getting money. Their experience was going to the synagogue, pay their tithe and enjoy the fellowship with other Jewish worshippers. Christ brought this to an end in a dramatic unexpected move. He took them to a future they did not experience. Jesus took them to a different world where life is completely different from that of the Galilean lifestyle of eating and dying. Here, Jesus taught them that He is the life Himself and whoever eats Him shall never die. He took them to a different map of the world breaking their narrow Galilean understanding and said here is your different map; the whole world and the world beyond the life they are experiencing.

The world beyond the life they were experiencing in Galilee was Christ Himself and they have seen, touched and interacted with Him. He, Jesus the different direction is taking them to a different walk of life which is completely different from the "Fishing around the Galilean sea." It is fishing from every sea in the world. The fishing is from East to West and from North to South. It is not stationed to the Galilean sea. The fishing boat is not that of "Zebedee's," but it is Christ Himself. Christ as the fishing boat is a guarantee for the disciples to go fishing.

Fishing in the Galilean sea was just for daily living and it was catching fishes to make them food. But here, the fishing was to bring fellow humans to the everlasting kingdom of the boat they are following; Christ. They do not need the nets of Peter nor that of Andrew nor that of Zebedee's children to catch fish here; they have the nets in their hands. It is Christ the word that catches fishes now. The only thing they do is disseminating the word that catches any fish and "make disciple" of Christ. It is a net that catches and "kills" fishes for a different life to let them begin a life coming out of death.

9. It involves a call into a different identity

According to Mark Mattes (2012, p.148) "it is not we but God who makes us Christ's disciples." This asserts that to be a disciple of Christ is a matter of call and it is not a matter of personal endeavor. It is not something earned. It is something given and does not mean something that an individual creates for himself/herself. The word "make" in Mattes (p. 148) is not a reference to the making of disciples, an assignment given to the church. The church is called to make disciples but that making itself is a matter of God's work through the church.

A new creation, the formation of a disciple is a matter of God's promise (Mattes, p. 143) and this promise forms disciples through the power of the word (p. 143). This word is the word that creates; it is the divine word, it is the word from the beginning without whom nothing was made as in John 1: 1–2: "In the beginning was the Word, and the Word was with God, and the Word was God. He was with God in the beginning."

A new creation is meant to be a new identity. This identity defines who we are in Christ. It displaces purpose in life. It is not a matter of gaining holiness; it is not a matter of striving to be holy, "it is a precise offering of one self to the cross" (Mattes, 2012, p. 148).

A cross depicts suffering and a disciple offers him/herself to the cross not because his/her suffering saves but because it depicts that to be true with God provokes opposition from the adversaries (p. 148). This is an identity to which a disciple is called. Mattes (p. 148) writes that a disciple's unique identity is a call into the "holy possession of the cross." It means that a student of Christ endures every suffering, persecution, poverty, sickness and whatever to be conformed into the likeness of Christ. Michael Brautigam (2019, p.70) strengthens this drawing our attention to what Luther said, "The true source of our identity is suffering and the cross of Christ." Brautigam (p. 70) writes basing his notion on Luther that we will obtain a true insight into who we really are, what our purpose in life is only "through suffering and the cross..." Jesus called his disciples into suffering and death as in Luke 14: 26–27 as follows:

> If anyone comes to me and does not hate father and
> mother, wife and children, brothers and sisters—
> yes, even their own life—such a person cannot be

my disciple. And whoever does not carry their cross
and follow me cannot be my disciple.

This text clearly elucidates that disciples are called to suffer not
by choice but by call and this call also separates the disciples into
a new identity; an identity born out of the unity in Christ. The
unity here is an identity of constant dying and rising with Christ.
Unless we constantly die with Christ we cannot be constantly raised.
This constant, uninterrupted death and resurrection with Christ
exemplifies that "we are deeply flawed beings" (Brautigam 2012,
p. 75). As we are committing deadly sins, it is only our unity in the
death and resurrection of Christ that helps us to recognize God and
justifies us by faith (p.75). According to Luther in Brautigam (p. 76)
we are "simulistus et peccator," living in a constant state of tension,
a constant dying and rising with Christ that strangles the old Adam
and puts a new self that grows in humility and love of God that is the
life only worth living (p. 76).

A true identity of the students of Christ stems from the suffering,
death and resurrection with Christ not as a life that saves, not as a
life to have better holiness but as a call into discipleship. This call
leaves a disciple or a student of Christ in a situation of prioritizing
Christ even in abandoning precious staff including our lives to walk
with him. By living their parents the disciples of Christ had chosen
the life of a cross, the life of suffering not as a supplement to be saved
through good works but as the children of God whose end is defined
solely by God, whose salvation is guaranteed on the basis of Christ,
we live in a constant fight.

6. It involves carrying a cross

According to Henerichsen (1988, p. 21) "nobody likes the cross.
Nobody likes to die. Nobody likes to deny himself. But this is what
the Lordship is all about." When Jesus calls you, every area of our lives
is under His jurisdiction (p. 21). We stand in defense of what Christ

wants than ours (p. 21). Since this over takes our choices, wants, needs and takes us to a complete surrender, it is painful and it is the cross which we do not like. Whether we like it or not, we are called to the carrying of a cross in Chris's Lordship. This over lordship of Christ entails that you cannot go without a cross ones you come to Christ.

Although anyone has a cross in life, this cross that a disciple carries is a cross that identifies him/her with Christ immediately after conversion. It is the sharing and the taking up of the passion of Christ in life. It is the road full of suffering as one follows Christ as a student in the kingdom. The cross is laid on a disciple once the person takes the walks of life with Christ. That cross produces death not as a terrible end of life but as an identity card of a disciple in the School of Christ (Bonhoeffer, 1959, p. 79).

The passion of Christ that a disciple takes into his/her life uniquely identifies the disciple with Christ. Bonhoeffer (1959, p. 80) declares that suffering is the badge of true discipleship. It is not only the product of following Christ but is a call into it as one enters the School of Christ. Following Christ, in the words of Bonhoeffer (p. 80) is "passio passivia" suffering because we have to suffer which Luther quoted in Bonhoeffer (p. 80) also asserted in the memorandum of the Augsburg confession depicting that suffering is among the marks of true church where true church references a true student of Christ.

7. It involves a conversion from blindness to sight

You cannot receive sight without recognizing and acknowledging that you are blind. Once you know your blindness you come to the one who gives you the sight. In truth anyone outside of Christ is blind regardless of a claim that he/she is not. A call to discipleship is a call from blindness to sight. It is an automatic divine conversion from the world of darkness and blindness into a world of light and sightedness.

Conversion and sight are automatic divine happenings in the life of a disciple. Be that as it may, the disciples of Christ were blind in their discipleship process and Jesus was trying to break through their blindness (Grannis, Laffin & Schade, 1981, p. 18). This notion asserts that sightedness in Christ is both automatic and a gradual process. A supporting notion to the gradual opening of one's sight is the Bethsaida man (John 5: 1-14).

The disciples of Christ were seeking greatness, dominance over the others, ambition for places of prestige and glory, opposition to the death of Christ as a ransom for the world while they were with Christ (Grannis, Laffin&Schade, 1981, p. 18). Every time Jesus was countering them, and they remained blind to the mission of Christ. It was a gradual process for them to come to true sightedness. The actual place to receive sightedness is at the cross of the suffering servant; Jesus Christ. Jesus' cross demands a journey; it demands unfamiliar terrains from Jerusalem to the cross (p. 21) a journey surrounded by many things that blind us. True sightedness comes by faith, it comes by a journey passing over the difficult life topographies and longing for the kingdom of God which is impossible without the transforming power of the cross (p. 21-22).

8. It involves a call into holistic ministry

Once a call is completed in the life of a disciple, the disciple begins to involve in holistic ministry. That ministry is the ministry of sharing the word and becoming vulnerable in the needs and services of others by walking in the path of the Cross. This idea displays that holistic ministry is a call and the result of the Cross. This holistic ministry is developmental, and it is the development of the whole man according to Walter A. Henerichsen (1988, p. 72). This development involves three areas; teaching, training and building in the words of Henerichsen (p. 73).

Teaching leads into training and training leads into building. Three of them are inseparably attached. To be trained one has to be taught and to be built one has to be trained. Building is holistic. Jesus was teaching, training and building his students throughout his ministries.

He did not simply teach or train but built them as holistic approach is unattainable without holistic ministry. Henerichsen (1988, p. 74) states that this building needs to encompass the intellectual, physical, spiritual and social developments. It means that students of Christ need to be equipped mentally and have knowledge of the word of Christ deeply indoctrinated, physically fit, spiritually connected to the Master Jesus in prayer, in Bible studies constantly but more in love. These all help the students of Christ in their relationship in a social environment. The students of Christ are not called to be out of the world, out of any social environment but live in the world, in any social environment without being conformed into the likeness of the world but use every opportunity existing among the society to reach them in Christ.

The teachings were involving focusing and observation which Greg Ogden (2003, p. 85) puts as the imitative stage. According to Ogden (p. 85) this imitative stage continued throughout the ministry of Christ. But in the early stages, the disciples were focusing and observing through asking questions to deeply know the person of Christ (p. 85). To support this, Ogden (p. 82) writes that they were asking who Jesus is, the nature of His ministry and mission. These all assert who the disciples were learning from to have true knowledge of who Jesus was.

According to Henerichsen (1988, p. 73) teaching is the imparting of knowledge. It is the transmission of knowledge from a teacher to a student. Knowledge is basically a deep understating of the scripture including key scriptural passages. Knowledge needs to be grown into skill that can be achieved through training.

According to Henerichsen (1988, p. 73) training is defined as the transfer of skill. It means a theoretical knowledge converted into skill. Skill involves techniques and techniques help to accomplish a result. These techniques are ways of starting conversation with someone who is not the child of Christ. This is a very important part in a secular environment that does not need Christ. Taking a cautious approach in talking about Christ and being equipped with techniques to reach out to people is a method that Christ developed.

Jesus was equipped in techniques to reach to others. For example in John 4: 1–42, as Jesus was talking to the Samaritan woman, the way He opened the conversation and finally won her for His kingdom is tantamount important. It was a normal conversation that grew into a strong unbreakable relationship that finally opened unthinkable heart and made surrender into the kingdom of God. The disciples of Christ need to be trained in this way to reach the lost people anywhere other than trying to proselyte others which also is an offence in some countries.

Training must be accompanied with building where building shows the true character of a person. It shows what a person looks like and what he/she looks like. It is a display of the fruits that one collects from trainings. If trainings do not produce the expected building, a building that is of fruits of acceptable standard, they are lost trainings.

Building is imparting of character. It is where individual students exhibit what they were taught and skilled in action. Fruits of their teachings and skills are shown here. Building produces character and character is a means by which anyone is measured. Teaching, learning, and training are futile attempts if they do not produce characters. People are made who they are by the characters they exhibit than their knowledge or learning or training skills. While knowledge, learning and trainings help people grow, they are like a tree without fruit if they are not accompanied with Character.

Any teaching (theoretical) must lead into practice and practice involves training

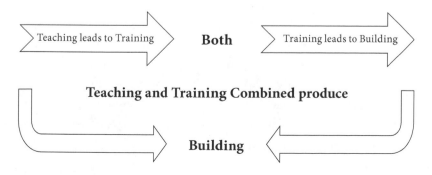

Teaching leads to Training   **Both**   Training leads to Building

Teaching and Training Combined produce

Building

Training leads to bearing fruits. Bearing fruits is the result of building. Without building which is based on the word of God to be fruitful is untenable.

9. A call to individualism

To understand a call to individualism in the context of Christ's studentship, one has to understand what it means first. Individualism can be defined as putting the interests of the individual above those of the group. In this context, it places the focus on what is best for "me," regardless of what effect that has on the "group." This type of individualism has no place in Christ's school of taught and among His disciples. Christ calls individuals and makes a church which is the community of believers and in the community of believers the interest of the group is above the interest of individuals.

The individualism that this book explains is an individual decision making to become the student of Christ. As such it elucidates faith individualism where an individual is required to personally and individually follow Christ. Faith individualism is a terminology that I coined based on religious individualism that Paul E. Davies discusses. In fact, both terms can be used interchangeably but I prefer faith individualism because my understanding is that faith is a gift and religion is a man-made science. Luther speaks of faith as a gift of God in his theology of Justification. Alister McGrath (1989, p. 17) quoting Luther puts it as follows:

> ...'Justification by faith', for Luther, does not mean that a sinner is justified on account of his faith, as if faith was a human work. It means that faith is a gift of God. Justification does indeed come about through faith - but that faith itself is a gracious gift of God, not a human action.

On the account of Luther's teaching, it is recommended to use the terminology faith individualism in this context. It is thus asserted that faith individualism is the core to follow Christ where an individual decides to follow Christ without the participation or a push from anyone. Bonhoeffer (1959, p. 84) explains that individuals decide by themselves. This decision comes out of their call to become individuals where they are called to be separated from their natural ties to follow alone (p. 84). Paul E. Davies (1956, p. 10) asserts this:

> The central requirement of faith is personal and individual. Men actually believe one by one, they are forgiven one by one-one by one they experience God's grace in justification, reconciliation, adoption. No mass movement is involved when Paul says, "As many as are led by the Spirit of God, these are the sons of God" (Rom. 8:14). Paul's difficult doc- trine of foreordination is centered on the individual, standing in the purpose of God.

In summary, Christ called His students to individually decide, to separate themselves from any external ties and follow Him. This was vivid in His call of His 1st disciples as in Matthew 4: 18–22 where the students departed from their conditions, family ties and individually decided to follow their Master, Jesus Christ. The call of Christ sets a barrier between the disciples/students/ "matheetees" of Christ and their natural ties (Bonheoffer, 1959, p. 85) where that barrier is an individual decision making to commit oneself to follow Christ. There was no group decision, mass movement in the students/ "matheetees" coming to that decision. It was an individual decision where we have become individuals for the sake of Christ (p. 90). This understanding in the words of Bonheoffer (p. 90) is summarized as students/disciples/ "matheetees" become individuals for Christ, left all at his call, and can say of themselves:

'Lo, we have left all, and followed thee,' which is the promise of a new fellowship. This fellowship is where individuals become a church, the fruit of Christ's death and resurrection. This avows that an individual or groups of individuals become a church which is a collective entity, thus an individual call becomes a collective call where the collective call is the body of Christ. The body of Christ is an aggregate of some individuals. Individuals come to Christ individually but live in the body of Christ without which a normal function is impossible.

The call into Christ's school can be depicted pictorially as follows:

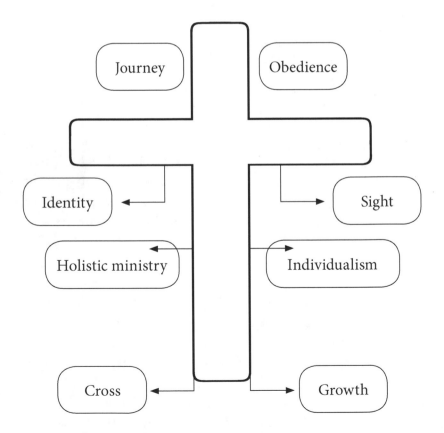

4

A Disciple (student) or A Christian

Are believers Christians?

One cannot speak about Christians without Christianity. Christians are the followers of the Christian faith and the source of the Christian faith according to "Cristo Redentor," in Mark Menzies (2015, p. 2) is one: the life, the teachings, the death, and the resurrection of Jesus. One may then ask did Jesus teach Christianity or did even Jesus use the "term Christians and Christianity" in His lifetime? The answer was simple; Jesus has never used the term Christians, and Christianity in His lifetime. The students of Christ also did not use the term Christians and Christianity. To that fact, the Christian scripture does not mention "Christianity" at all until after the Pentecost Sunday. It mentions the followers of Christ as the followers, the disciples, the believers. Astoundingly, the Christian scripture mentions the term Christians only three times with the term first in history mentioned and used at Antioch in the Asian minor according to Acts 11: 26, "The disciples were called Christians first at Antioch."

The term Christians was applied to the followers of Christ, the students that Jesus produced in his life time. It was applied to the students only after Jesus ascended into heaven and the church was born. The term was not the choice of the students of Christ. It was neither the choice of their Master and it was a derogatory term applied to the students as a means of mocking and ridiculing them.

According to Dennis Hinks (2003, p. 3) "originally, the word "Christian" was a term of derision that enemies of Jesus labeled His followers. It was intended as an insult or mockery." Hinks (p. 1) states that "instead of being a compliment - or even a status symbol (as it sometimes is, today) - it was an insult. "A status of symbol," which Hinks (p.1) mentions here attests that Christianity was in fact imitation; it is following one who is unique in history that strongly influenced His followers.

A status symbol is of course not earned in the Christian faith, it is something bestowed upon a believer. According to Erving Goffman (2003, p. 295-296) status symbol is worn and it shows the rank of a person. Goffman (p, 296) writes that "status symbol is distinct and separates a person who wears showing the status of the claimant," in this case, a Christian or a follower of the Lord. One argues that if to be called a Christian is a status symbol, it is displayed and it is seen by observers where it signifies that a Christian is a completely different person in his/her identity- this notion accurately describes what a student of Christ or a disciple is meant but does the Christians of today and the past centuries truly show the calling of their faith?

According to Anderson & Skinner (2019, p. 66) Christ calls believers to be disciples. That means every believer is called to be a student, a disciple and there is no other alternative. Anderson & Skinner (p. 67) also state that these students are "spirit filled Christians." That means both to be a "disciple" and to be a "spirit filled Christian" are the same.

The phrase "Spirit filled Christian," was not a phrase neither coined by Jesus nor applied by Jesus to His followers. Although who coined the phrase for the 1st time is obscured, it is doubted from where and how Anderson & Skinner (p. 67) used the terminology as the same as a "disciple. It is unscientific to disqualify Anderson's notion of understanding here but it brings the idea of "non-Spirit filled Christian" or a "Christian" as opposed to "Spirit filled Christian." It is avowed from this that one has to be a spirit filled Christian to be a true student of Christ or a disciple.

The measurement for someone who claims "Spirit filled "in contrast to a "non- spirit filled Christian / Christian is yet to be discussed. This assertion states that there are two types of people that claim the name Christianity. According to Thomas A. Tarrants (2014, p. 2) this creates confusion if Jesus offered two acceptable standards of living the Christian life. Tarrants (p. 2) explains that these two Christian lives are the one which is less demanding- ordinary Christian life and an optional, more challenging version for those who commit themselves to be the disciples or students of Christ. This means that the "less demanding Christian life- the ordinary one-as inferred from its name depicts the notion that one is not bound to live a wholehearted discipleship life for Christ. It elucidates a nominal way of life immersed into the worldly life to the extent of inseparability where a Christian of less demanding Christian life lives the same life with those who do not belong to Christ. These groups that possess less demanding Christian life are those that are not the disciples of Christ. Jesus did not teach Christianity nor Spirit filled Christianity nor non-spirit filled way of living the life of His calling. Jesus called everyone to be a student for a lifetime.

The more challenging version of Christianity as Tarrant (2014, p. 2) states is the one that demands wholehearted living for Christ. Two things raise questions here. The first is that it is more challenging. Jesus did not call anyone into a challenging life style as a life that is demanded from a believer. Jesus gave His life and He wanted each and every follower to live this life as a student- a learner in progressing.

A student of Christ is called into studentship that his/her call is in an unending session that takes every day and time to grow- that is a growth into Christ. There is no challenge here; there is only life that a student is to live. Unlike Tarrant (p. 2) the life to which the student of Christ is called is neither less nor optional nor more challenging but it is the life of the cross and it is not a new experience out of the blue. It is the experience of a Master to the students. It is a life full of Christ and a life with Christ.

The second is what Tarrant (2014, p. 2) states as a "wholehearted living." The students of Christ live a "wholehearted living," not because they aspire it or the life with Christ required of them. It is what any justified believer lives because he/she is justified on the account of Christ. This living does not justify nor makes the students of Christ more holy but it is a fruit coming out of the justified life.

In summary, Jesus called His student (s) to be a student (s) no less or no greater. To be a student is an automatic occurrence in the life of a believer immediately he/she is saved. The road of a studentship yet is a process. To be a student of the Lord has nothing to do with "spirit filled or none Spirit filled," as a disciple or a student gains the power of a student of Christ immediately when saved. This power is the power of authority, an instant manifestation in the life of a believer when he/she received Him. John 1: 12–13 affirms:

> Yet to all who did receive him, to those who believed in his name, he gave the right to become children of God— [13] children born not of natural descent, nor of human decision or a husband's will, but born of God.

Rwandan-ism: A violent Christianity

Rwandan-ism is the term I coined in reference to a violent genocidal killing that took place in Rwanda in 1994. The killings were at most between two ethnic groups; the Hutu and Tutsi and at most among the dominant Christian religion followers belonging to both the Hutu and Tutsi without any ethnic divide. According to Lee C. Camp

(2008, p. 19) Christians make up 90 percent of the total population in Rwanda. Camp (p. 19) also describes Rwanda as "the most Christian country in Africa." These Christians were the result of immense work of the Western missionaries and yet Camp (p. 20) describes the gospel that reached the Rwandese as the "imported gospel."

The "imported gospel" refers to the notion that the gospel in Rwanda was not an inborn Rwanda Christianity from the Rwandan Christians but a reference to the Western Missionaries dissemination of the Christian faith in Rwanda. Whether the Christian faith in Rwanda was imported or sprang up from among the Rwandese, "Christianity as such bear an important responsibility for the Rwandan genocide," according to Timothy Longman (2010, p. 667). Longman (p. 667) argues that the distinct nature of Christianity in Rwanda as it developed over time made genocide morally possible: Longman (p. 667) writes that, "the Christian message received in Rwanda was not one of "love and fellowship", but one of obedience, division, and power".

As a country mostly inhabited by Christians, it is undoubted that Christians take the largest share in the involvement of the genocidal killings. This raises a question of the message of Christianity preached among the Rwandese which Longman argued as missing the message of love and fellowship, a central theme of the Christian faith. NicCheeseman writes (2010, p. 670):

> That massive participation of Christians in the genocide was a consequence of the fact that Christianity had not taken deep root in Rwandan society. But the puzzle of the Rwandan genocide is not only why the majority of ordinary (Christian) Rwandans could become involved in the genocide, but especially why they actually were involved in the killing of their neighbors.

"In the killings of their neighbor," is a violation of the ten commandments of God where believers are called to love their God and their neighbors as themselves. The message of love contained in the ten commandments other than observing them, other than confessing them other than reciting them and memorizing them as a creed to show that one is a believer did not bear fruit of love in Rwanda where a neighbor took a sword against his/her neighbor purchased by the cross of Christ.

In general, the Rwandan Christianity was not that of discipleship, it was not a Christianity that led believers to be the true students of Christ built on the love of Christ to love their brothers/sisters irrespective of their ethnic identity, cultural background and linguistic make up. It was a Christianity built on the message of division, power, glory and hatred of those different from "us." The message of the cross is always and forever be the message of love and fellowship regardless of the differences we have on this planet. The church is the church of diverse groups of people where the kingdom of God operates in love and in fellowship.

To sum up, Rwandan-ism is not confined to a single geographic environment. It is disseminated over the globe where people preach power, glory, division, and obedience in the absence of the fruits of love. The core element of the teachings of Christ is love beyond ethnic identity, a search for glory and power. It is all about I am because we are. The true teaching of Christ helps one to grow in love rooted in the person of Christ. A student/ disciple in the school of Christ is a called individual who always stands against Rwandan-ism, a power and division driven Christianity.

Cultural Christianity

The Got questions blog (2015) defines cultural Christianity as a "religion that superficially identifies itself as "Christianity" but does not truly adhere to the faith." It is best described as syncretism where a culture and the Christian belief are blended together to the point where the follower of the Christian faith does not adhere to its teachings.

In cultural Christianity, the label Christian is exhibited in the life of the follower. In such case according to Leo Tolstoy in Camp (2008, p. 27) "there is no way to tell from the persons past, there is no way to tell from a person's life, from his deeds, whether or not he is a believer." Camp (p. 27) describes this type of Christianity as "dubbed "Christian," and yet is un-Christ like." In such Christianity, biblical emphasis on discipleship is replaced with religious rituals and salvation is seen as a fire insurance policy, a ".....Free Card," guaranteeing an escape from fires of torment and ensuring the receipt of treasures in heaven (P. 27).

Camp's (2008, p. 27) understanding of the "receipt of treasurers in heaven" describes salvation of such Christians as something guaranteed and unguaranteed. It is guaranteed because it details that escape from torment is guaranteed yet unguaranteed because the receipt is going to be handed into the believers hands in the future. This counters the theology of salvation as salvation is now and believers are surely guaranteed of their salvation on the account of Christ.

The church from its inception has been in culture and cannot be on a separate Island. It operates in cultures, bringing souls to Christ from diverse cultures nurturing its members to be transformed not into cultures but into the likeness of Christ. This nurturing attests that the church continues to teach its members to be true students of Christ through studentship. Unlike the call of the church, Christianity is transformed into cultures and most Christians do not even know a dividing line between their culture and their Christian faith. Tom Strode (2016) states that Christians need to learn not only how to engage the culture in a gospel-focused manner, but also avoid becoming a captive of cultural Christianity

Camp (2008, p. 21) taking the State of Alabama in the US and describes it as the most Christian area with Nashville as the most Christian city; the Protestant Vatican, the Jerusalem of Christians as it is heritage elucidates that the area is featured by unrepentant, blinded by unredeemed cultural forces that leave believers prey to forces and principalities of this world and lack of discipleship and thus not different from the failed Rwandan Christianity.

The notion that "lack of discipleship," is exhibit attests that the Christian faith does not go anywhere in its mission as it lacks the core teaching of the New Testament. Jesus called everyone to be a student in His Kingdom and continue in the paths of studentship.

Jesus did not call anyone to be a cultural Christian nor a Christianity that preaches division and aspiration, a longing for power but of love and fellowship. Jesus did not call anyone nor teach that people who come to Him become anything other than students in His school for a life time where growth in the knowledge and grace is pouring. This growing in the grace of Christ is nothing other than growing in love that includes our actions, thoughts, and behaviors. In this growth, the students of Christ grow within culture but not in transformation into a cultural make up of the world. The students of Christ are born in cultures, grow and live but not entangled with the many evils coming out of the world cultures. The students of Christ use every divine ingredient in cultures for the glory of Christ.

Emotion driven Christianity

According to Marika Mitchell (2004, p. 1) "there is no human being without emotion." That means all are created with emotions. Mitchell (2004, p. 1) quoting Copeland writes, "the capacity to feel and express emotions is a wonderful gift from God ..." God not only created humans with emotions He also shares the full range of human emotions according to Jackson in Mitchell (2004, p. 1). According to Wilson in Mitchell (2004, P. 3), the word is derived from the Latin "emovere," meaning to move. According to Meyer in Mitchell (2004, p.1) emotions are "a complex, usually strong subjective response involving physiological changes as a preparation for action".

Mitchell (2004, p.1) states that after man's fall in sin, emotions became self-directed and out of control. Mitchell (p.1) quoting Meyer writes that carnal, uncrucified emotions try to lure people away from or out of the will of God. "Carnal and un-'crucified'," are words taken from the Bible.

Carnal means someone who is in a childish stage when he/she is to be an adult. It states that someone is not living up to his/her ages. Carnal individuals are immature and they are not growing. The lack of growth exhibits that there is unhealthy situation in the life of a person. Carnality is a condition and an act. It is an act in the situation when a carnal person is trapped in sin and fall. It is a condition when the carnal person stays in the situation longer. "Longer," here states that the person commits sin again and again without exhibiting the life of repentance. The longer he/she continues to repeatedly rebel against God, the more dragged into leaving the fellowship with Christ. Such believers are usually emotional. They are driven by their emotions, pretend that they are fully converted, or they are converted but began to be constantly rebelling against the word of God. They look clean but do not exhibit the fruits of the spirit. Although he is against, I quote Ernest C. Reisinger (1978, p.1) who states that Carnal,

> Regularly occupy church pews, fill church rolls, and are intellectually acquainted with the facts of the gospel never strike one blow for Christ. They seem to be at peace with his enemies. They have no quarrel with sin and, apart from a few sentimental expressions about Christ; there is no biblical evidence that they have experienced anything of the power of the gospel in their lives.

Uncrucifed is the opposite of Crucified. According to Luis Cilliers (2003, p.938) crucifixion is defined as a method of execution by which a person is hanged, usually by his arms from across or similar structures until he dies. Jesus was crucified on the cross, and He was killed in a brutal killing unprecedented in human history. Paul states:

"I have been crucified with Christ and I no longer live, but Christ lives in me. The life I now live in the body, I live by faith in the Son of God, who loved me and gave Himself for me," Galatians 2: 20.

In saying this, Paul explains that Jesus did not die alone but He died with all of us. This does not mean that we paid the price nor Paul paid but the price was paid by Christ on behalf of us. If Paul or anyone of us died on the cross or crucified, it means that we are contributing to our salvation and that disqualifies the theology of our salvation which states that we are saved by grace on the account of Christ. Robert Kolbe (1993, p. 145) writes that God is pleased only with whom He makes His children apart from any performance of their own. But what does to be crucified with Christ mean? It means that the penalty was fully paid attesting that we were crucified for our own sin. We were also buried with Christ and rose with Him. In being buried with Him our sins were also buried (Kolbe p. 145).

As we are resurrected, we live by the power of Christ to live the life that pleases Him not a life driven by emotions whether emotions are important or not. In our worship and actions; in words or in deeds, we live the life that pleases the Lord. This life is not a life driven by emotions but a life driven daily by the death and resurrection of Christ. Our calling exemplifies our death and resurrection with Christ and not a life of emotions. According to Bonheoffer (1959, p. 79), "When Christ calls a man He bids him to come and die." Death here is a death to carnal emotions and uncrucified lifestyle as uncrucified has no place in the kingdom of Christ. If uncrucified is exhibited in the life of believers, it is their choice and not their calling.

A believer's call is to come and die. This coming and dying is crucifixion. Crucifixion produces a new person in Christ. A new person shows the death of the Old with its corrupted, carnal and uncrucified emotions. The new person then begins a new walk with Christ. Paul in Romans 6: 4 states, "We were therefore buried with Him through baptism into death in order that, just as Christ was raised from the dead through the glory of the Father, we too may live a new life." This notion avows that any old life with all its desires including emotions that drag us to a wrong life style, a pretending life style; a lifestyle driven by emotions not knowledge and wisdom are uncrucified. Uncrucified life style of any form is not the quality of true students of Christ. Uncrucified emotion, as stated, is also not a life quality of a newborn person in Christ.

Crucified as opposed to uncrucified, shows a life of new commitment, dedication to services and glory of the Lord. Such dedications destroy selfishness, ties of any kind that does not put Christ first. In uncrucified life driven by emotion, it is self-interest, self-glory, personal ties that take the priority. In uncrucified life style, the cross is lucking. Luke 14: 27 states, "And whoever does not carry their cross and follow me cannot be my disciple." Then cross subdues our emotion, feelings and any carnal move from Christ and connects us to Christ. Students of Christ carry their own cross that always puts Christ the priority in life. And when Christ is the priority, there is no room for carnal and uncrucified life.

To sum up, there is no one without emotion. There is also divine truth that human emotion is corrupted by fall but redeemed by Christ for His glory. Any unredeemed part of our studentship in Christ, attest that carnal-ism and the power of emotion have taken root. The students of Christ are united with Christ in His death and resurrection. They are new creatures whose old life including corrupted emotion is buried forever. In a generation where emotion is significantly exhibit in every aspect of life, the students of Christ need to control their emotion and display Christ as their own emblem. As an emblem carried, worn and displayed, Christ is the one whose glory masks, subdues and kills every emotion that takes His place in our walk with Him as students for a lifetime.

The Music driven generation

Photo Credit: the author

Music is a powerful weapon to reach the unreached, edify those who are believers. That means Music teaches the gospel of Christ. Martin Luther in Delton L. Alford (1967, p, 70) stated the value of Music as follows: "...the devil flees before the sound of music almost as much as before the word of God." John Huss the great reformer quoted in Alford (p. 70) also stated the significance of Music in 1415 as follows: "We preach the gospel not only from the pulpit but also from hymns."

Music conveys a powerful message into the heart of people. It transcends circumstances and speaks to people. Caleb Brasher (2015) states that "Music can not only take us back to moments in our past, it can also conjure up emotion in our present," and even speak to the future.

Music through which the gospel reaches to the people is a gift than an art. It is profoundly argued that Music comes from the Holy Spirit. The notion that the Holy Spirit is the source of Music among believers concludes that Music is "Theo-Centric." The Scripture also affirms that Music is led by skillful men who were sanctified (1 Chronicles 15: 22). One cannot be sanctified without the Holy Spirit. David C. McCasland (2016) states about Music as follows:

> Music is deeply rooted in our souls. And for the followers of Jesus, it is a powerful means of encouraging each other along the journey of faith.

Paul urged the believers in Colossae, "Let Christ's teaching live in your hearts, making you rich in the true wisdom. Teach and help one another along the right road with your psalms and hymns and Christian songs, singing God's praises with joyful hearts" (Col. 3:16 Phillips). Singing together to the Lord embeds the message of His love in our minds and souls. It is a powerful ministry of teaching and encouragement that we share together. Whether our hearts cry out, "Create in me a pure heart, O God" (Ps. 51:10), or joyfully shout, "And he will reign forever and ever" (Rev. 11:15), the power of music that exalts God lifts our spirits and grants us peace.

The creation of a pure heart is not a human endeavor. It is totally a divine operation and the act of the word of God. This divine operation makes believers spiritual and spiritual people generate spiritual Music.

Music from believers is not for emotional or motivational purposes. Although emotion and motivation are not avoided in any music, the main objective of music in Christian worship is to show our submission and complete surrender to God. Thus, the purpose of Music in Christianity is submission to God. Contrary to this, Brasher (2015) writes that many churches create an emotional experience each Sunday through musical worship and pawn it as an experience of the Holy Spirit. Brasher (2015) says that countless of multitudes leave the church crying believing that they have experienced God but it was not God but an emotion similar to a boy in the back seat of a car crying to his parents. This notion states the power of emotion and how it manipulates the truth. In fact, Brasher's (2015) argument is a generalization and it is highly disputed to conclude all "crying" in the church is the result of an emotion than the touch of Christ. Brasher's thought put Christ as absent when Christ is truly among His students touching, healing and drawing them to Himself.

Music in the church must bring people into true worship, root them in the scripture, lead them to prayer and connect them to God. It must counter emotions that drag people from the Lord and the word. Basher (2015) writes:

> The words we sing and proclaim are far more important than the way we feel. As a good friend of mine has said, "Content is king. Creativity and catchiness are its faithful servants." So let your heart be led by objective truth and not by subjective and fleeting emotion.

The students of Christ are not called to be Music driven. They are called to be students/ disciples. They may adopt any method including Music to reach to the unreached, edify those churched but are called to be students committed to carry Christ as their Lordship. They are called to abide in the word. The students' of Christ are sure that abiding by the words of Christ makes them true disciples. Without the word and without living the word, to be a disciple and discipleship is unattainable. John 8: 31 states, "Then said Jesus to those Jews which believed on Him, if ye continue in my word, then are my disciples indeed."

One yet observes the flaws within the Music driven generation. First, the Music driven generation mostly writes Music only because the sounds are welcoming but not the words. That means the words are not scriptural and at times theologically unsound, grammatically incorrect and the flows are not passing the same message. A typical example to this is, Music from Ethiopia and for that matter this section discusses Ethiopian Spiritual Music.

Second, Music is mostly for competition and not to reach to others with the message of love and fellowship. This competition is driven from the notion that a beautiful Music, a well arranged Music, a Music with modern Musical instruments and a Music that captures peoples' mind and heart is a way for success. This success is success in terms of getting more stages to sing, more popularity and more money. In general, it is all about a move to be "great among the others," that counters the words of Christ. In Matthew 20: 26 Jesus taught how one becomes great and stated, "Not so with you. Instead, whoever wants to become great among you must be your servant."

In the school of Christ, one cannot be great or better by competition, by service or gaining popularity but by living the life of humility, love and the cross. In running for popularity, Ethiopian Christian singers and the Ethiopian Music industry has paved the way for rampant business competition where the success of the other leads to the failure of the other. In such move it has systematically transformed itself into a rush for blessings but not Christ.

Third, the Music driven generation has mostly converted itself into a commercial entity where it seeks to gain profit from the production of church based songs. In changing itself into a commercial entity, individuals seek to control the market than bring people to Christ. As it is market based, the words of the songs are usually articulated perfectly to gain audiences and amass money and popularity.

In all, Music driven generation are believers with a different mindset- a mind set on popularity, commercialization and fame. These all are not features of the true students of Christ. For the students of Christ, their popularity is Christ, their fame comes from humility, and their food is the provider Christ. Jesus did not teach His students to be converted into the likeness of the world for such likenesses are a run to be popular, a rush to gain economic profit. In fact, Jesus did not teach that believers should not work, seek success or popularity but He taught that the sole call of a student is to glorify, adore, and make Jesus the mark of his/her life anywhere anytime

Data Analysis

The Study and the selection criteria: The study is based on library materials and an interview conducted among members of the Ethiopian community assumed to be communicant members of their church. The study captures Biblical foundations for the call of students to be the true students of Christ, what a student life looks like in terms of exhibiting the fruits of the students of Christ. The study also captures and compares what a Christian is meant about versus to a student of Christ. References were properly cited and interviewees were categorized into different denominations, gender and age discrepancy.

In the age category, the boys and girls are teenagers and the men and women are adults who are communicants in a church. Based on their understanding they are also divided into those who claim to be Christians, students/disciples or both or do not know.

Results: The majority of the interviewees are between 15 and 50 years of age. The interviewees are divided into boys, girls, men and women on the basis of age. There is no demographic disparity among the interviews. A total of 238 individuals were interviewed. Among these both men and women make 29.41% each. The girls make up 18.49. The boys make 22.69%. Disparity in number does not reflect any significant difference in their understanding of what a Christian and a student/disciple is meant about.

Categories of the claimants: Among 238 interviewees 13.3 % claim to be a student/disciple. 13.44 claim to be both Christians and disciples. This means they do not have any preference in name but detail that a Christian and a student/ a disciple are the same. The big majority, about 65.97 claim that they are Christians and do not want to be called a disciple or a student. 7.56 % do not know whether they are called Christians or students/disciples.

Description	Interviewed	Claim Christian	Claim disciple	Christian & Disciple	Do not know
Boys	54	25	10	9	10
Girls	44	27	6	7	4
Men	70	50	10	10	0
women	70	55	5	6	4
Total	238	157	31	32	18

Key Time Periods: This interview was conducted at different places in Washington, DC, Maryland & Virginia during different times between 2018 and April 2020.

Geographic origin: The interviewees are located in Washington, DC, Virginia, and Maryland. Majority of them are born in Ethiopia and participate in the Ethiopian worship system. Those that represent the boys and girls category are mostly born in the US and do not have much about what a Christianity in Ethiopia is. Yet they are pastored under pastors of Ethiopian origin.

Discussion: According to my findings elucidated in this data majority of the Ethiopian Evangelical Church MekaneYesus (EECMY) members claim to be Christians followed by the Ethiopian Full Gospel Believers church (EFBC) members and the Ethiopian Meserete Kristos Church (MKC). The Ethiopian Kale Hiwot Church (EKC) comes in the last row. Although this data reflects diversity in the claimants, it does not totally attest that those believers in Ethiopia consider themselves accordingly. It is my at most belief that believers in Ethiopia claim to be Christians. My reason is that those who are immigrants and those dwelling in the US could not represent the majority of Christians in Ethiopia. But it is argued that when it comes to those claiming a student or a disciple, my conclusion is that it is a matter of their exposure that impacted their view. It is added that as many of these immigrants are better off in education compared to those in Ethiopia, exposure to religious education, sermons and books have impacted their view to claim to be a "Student/Disciple." The claim to be a student depicts a lifelong process, an attachment and an undetached relationship with Christ. It is an automatic occurrence once a person is saved and it a learning process in the school of Christ.

In fact, it is Biblical to claim to be a student or a disciple, for Christ did not call anyone to be anything other than this. Christianity and the name Christian were given to the disciples by none Christians and it was not the choice of the disciples. Christ was not the founder of any religion and did not give any name to His disciples other than calling them, "My Disciples/Students." Jesus also gave His life and He was the authorship of the life of salvation in the His students/disciples.

The disparity among the claimants to be called the students/disciples of Christ or to be called Christians has broad implication to my knowledge. First, it rests on the exposure to theological training centers or Seminaries in Ethiopia and how the members of the different denominations are pastored. Theological trainings/Seminaries on the call of a student/disciple is vital and lessons offered at the theological training centers and seminaries are tantamount vital in shaping the life of a believer as a student and towards studentship. This data attests that most members of the EECMY preferred to be called Christians. A total of 10.08% of the EECMY among the interviewees of 238 claim to be Christians, in addition to 8.40% who claim to be called a Christian or a student /disciple. Both groups that claim a Christian and a Christian/a student category makeup 18.49%.

To make a conclusion from this, it is asserted that many EECMY members claim to be Christians. The notion that they claim to be called a "Christian" and at times claim to be called a "student/disciple" does not reflect the lifestyle of the claimants. But one is assured that they witness Christ and have strong relationships with Christ in their daily lives which conclude that true Christians are the students of Christ. At most this is shaped by their theological foundations that resulted from their pastoral background. Their pastoral background resulted from the theological seminaries/trainings from where their pastors grasped education. Thus, education is vital in shaping our Christian life as true Christians or to be true students of Christ.

Second, basic biblical trainings offered towards members of a certain congregation or denomination impacts their Christian life. It roots them in Christ, impacts their daily life towards producing the fruits of the spirit and live a life of the student of Christ. It even impacts their name preference where those who were truly rooted in the divine word call themselves the students of Christ. To be called a "student or a disciple" is thus an identity. It is an identity generated from one's life rooted in the divine word. Without the divine word which is the source of the call of a student, it is impossible to claim the name.

The divine word of Christ produces identity in a person. That identity is an identity in the name itself where the name bears the name of a person who branded it. Jesus is the name brand of a student. A student never exists without Christ in the school of Christ and Jesus is the one calls and who names a follower to be a student. Jesus is the one who calls a student to himself and He is the "preincarnate" word by whom everything is made. The identity of the person called to be a follower as a student for a lifelong is thus an identity of a permanent walk with Christ.

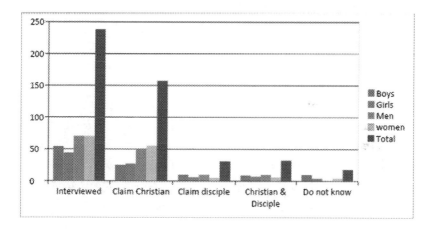

The numbers of interviewees that claim to be called students/disciples within the EECMY are 7.14% out of the 238 (members of different denominations) people reached out for interview. The implication is that should a large majority of the EECMY are interviewed; the number may rise and attest that preference to be called a "student/disciple" within the EECMY is growing. Also, the notion that their life style is growing towards their call as a student is vivid. Without living the life of a student/disciple, it is concluded that those who claim the name are nominals. The measurement for the life of a student is living Christ, obedience to His words, reflecting everything in action and in words for the glory of Christ. This meant that as a student in the school of Christ, a student grows, at times stumbles, blinded and even fails to comprehend Christ but never quits. That was exactly who the disciples of Christ were in their walk with Him.

The other denominations as seen from the graph below vary in their understanding of what to be called a "Christian" or a "student" is meant about. Members of different denominations differ in percentage. This difference does not by any means reflect the life that they have in Christ. Some of them do not have any knowledge of what to be called a "student/disciple" or a "Christian" is partly because they do not have ample knowledge of Biblical understanding. They learned discipleship but do not have any knowledge of why Jesus called all His followers "students/disciples" and not Christians. They do not have any clue that the call to be a student is inseparable from an instant salvation of a person in Christ. Their understanding is that one becomes a better student/disciple in a process but that is a complete misunderstanding of what "discipleship and student/disciple" is meant about. Discipleship is a process but one becomes a student/disciple upon his/her call. Once a person becomes a student/disciple, he/she continues to be in a discipleship process- a studentship which is a process of growing in Christ, getting deep rooted and growing in faith.

Denominations	Christians	Both Christian and Disciples	Disciples	Do not know	Total
EECMY	24	20	17	4	
EFBC	25	16	8	4	
EKC	17	16	8	7	238
EMC	20	20	10	5	
Others	2	2	2	3	

Denominational Category

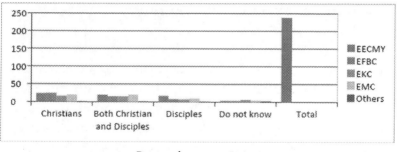

Bar graph representation

The discrepancy in response emanated from two reasons. First, as the data depicts some stated that they are Christians, others answered that they are students/disciples and others claimed both while few respondents did not even know. The responses attest that knowledge of the scripture is lacking. The lack of knowledge even goes to how the believers are pastored which puts the question on the pastors themselves. The pastors' knowledge of the scripture and teaching ability matters how a believer lives, reacts, and how the believer doctrinally explains his/her name which shows the identity of a person. If a believer does not know his/her name correctly, is not able to describe his/her identity, the problem rests not only on the believers lack of knowledge which rests on the believer him/herself but also how the pastors teach certain significantly important doctrinal issues about being the student/ disciple of Christ.

Second, it is because of lack of appropriate teaching which results from lack of basic theological trainings from pastors. A pastor is not only someone who feeds his/her members but has to be passed through certain advanced theological training to correctly feed or produce sound doctrines about the students of Christ and shape the life of his/her members towards the true teachings of Christ.

The Need for Theological Training

According to Ashish Chrispal (2019) "theology is for the whole church." This asserts that theology is not for theologians only. It is not for the few elitists (2019). That means it is not for those theologians who attended theological schools but it is for the whole members of the church. The New Testament writers also avowed that the church needs to be rooted in the word of God (Col. 2: 6-7). The church here designates the entire members of the church. If the members of the church are rooted in the word, they know their identity, who they are, what they believe and what they witness. These are in fact qualities of a student of Christ.

A student of Christ is not called neither by emotions, nor by personal feelings, ideologies and doctrines but called by the divine word of Christ. This word is a divine word and it is where they are grounded. The word that calls a student is a unique identity and a whole history of the student of Christ. To address the need for theological training, I would like to take three points of Elijah Otokola (2017, p. 93-94):

First, Christ-centered education puts salvation first. Christ is the center of life and the message of Christian education (Otokola, 2017, p. 93-94). This acetifies that education is important but education comes after a student is ready to learn. In the context of Christ, the student's salvation comes first. Both Salvation and the status of a person to be a student are automatic occurrences. They are inseparable as one becomes a student of Christ at a time when he/she is saved. Education follows after wards. In the other context, education may lead someone to salvation. In both cases whether salvation comes before or after the salvation of a person, it is a divine act. No one saves him/herself. Salvation in its entirety depends on Christ. The salvation of a student whether after resuming a certain education in faith or without resuming is a divine operation.

Christ-centered education recognizes that the child is basically evil (Otokola 2017, p. 93-94): That may sound like a strong statement, but a study of God's Word makes it very clear as to the condition of the human heart (Jer. 17:9; Eph. 2:1-3). It is not the environment that causes the discipline problems in the child, it is the sin nature (p. 93-94). People sin because they are sinners. They practice sin and live in self-will and self-centeredness. The heart needs a drastic change that takes place through salvation by faith in Christ's death on the cross (I Tim. 1:15; Prov. 22:15; Psa. 51: 5; Psa. 53; 58:3; Eph. 2:1-3). Only the child that is rightly related to Jesus Christ can receive the full benefits of a Christian education (Rom. 6:16-20).

Second, public education is thoroughly pupil-centered (Otokola 2017, p. 93-94). Self-esteem is often the basis of much false teaching in many schools, where the student is taught directly and indirectly to be selfish, self-centered. Instead of Christ-esteem, it is worship of self, the deifying of man (p. 93-94). Christ-centered education teaches Christ and His claims upon the lives of the students. The student ought not to have selfish rights of his own for once he is saved he belongs to Jesus. We are bought with a price, we are not our own (I Cor. 6:19-20). We are to yield our bodies to Christ. (Rom. 6:13; 12:1-2)

Third, Christ-centered education states that the content for Christian education must be in harmony with the teachings of the Bible (II Tim. 3:16-17; Psa. 119:128; Psa. 119) (Otokola (2017, p. 93-94). This provides the basis for the integration and correlation of all subject matter (p. 93-94). Every subject is taught with Christ as the center. Instruction takes on new meaning when the subjects are interpreted in the light of the Word of God. What does God say? History becomes the story of God's dealing with mankind (p. 93-94).

To sum up, theology impacts students, shapes them and takes them to the right direction in their Christian lives. It also roots them in true Biblical understanding, makes them grow as students with no alternative as Christ said, "You are my disciples," John 8: 31. There is no way to be a disciple/ as a student without clinging to the word of Christ and even Christ Himself as His words and Christ are inseparable.

Conclusion

According to Gary C. Newton in Shirely (2012, p. 208) a disciple is a learner; the Greek word "matheetees" is the root of our word mathematics, which means "thought accompanied by endeavor." This does not simply mean the flow of information into a student of Christ. Jesus was teaching his students that He is the eternal word, He is the kingdom, and He is the alpha and Omega. In all He taught them that He was the life with no alternative in place and they were living in a copy paste type of the life of their Master- Jesus Christ and that was above information transfer.

Learning is a process and it is not completed within a given period of time. The disciple of Christ learns always. The word Student/ Disciple occurs 258 times in the New Testament where 230 times in the Gospels and 28 times in the book of Acts (Shirley, 2008, p.208). This also shows how vital to be a student of Christ is in the scripture and there is no other choice to be a follower of Christ. No other name replaces being the student of Christ although the followers of Christ are called by different names depending on how they are oriented in different cultures. To this, the name given to the disciples after the ascension of Jesus and after the birth of the church in the book of acts 11:26 is the best example. Here the students of Christ were called for the 1st time Christians which was an alien name, a name of not their choice, a name imposed on them by none believers but became a brand of who the apostles were in the process of time and a universal name by which all believers in the world are known.

According to Wilkins in Chris Shirley (2008, p. 209) the qualifications for true disciples were: (1) Belief in Jesus as messiah (John 2:11, 6:68–69); (2) Commitment to identify with Him through baptism; (3) Obedience to his teaching and submission to his Lordship (Matt 19:23–30, Luke 14:25–33). These three qualifications rest on the 1st qualification as one cannot be a disciple without believing in Jesus. The believing asserts that there is no salvation without it. There never exists a disciple without salvation. This also reiterates that to be a disciple and to be saved are inseparable. In fact, it explicates that a disciple is before discipleship. While discipleship is a growth process, to be a disciple is an automatic gift in the life of a believer. Contrary to Shirley (2008, p. 209) where she writes that "commitment to identify with Him through baptism" as a second event in the life of a believer or a student of Christ, my theological upbringing asserts that baptism is where to be a disciple begins and as such salvation begins in baptism that marks the resumption of a new life in a believer as a student. While I stand in contrast to Shirley (p. 209) here, it is my firm belief that to be a student of Christ and the salvation of a student are automatic simultaneous occurrences.

Learning is an environment where we experience differences. These differences are many in nature but our differences are united in the Lord Jesus Christ. We are different in many ways as the twelve disciples were completely different attesting that the school of Christ is a school of diverse people. Their diversity yet did not impact their fellowship; it did not create any compromise on their commitment with Christ and service.

Learning is also an environment where people grow in knowledge, wisdom and grace. The student of Christ is called to grow and growth is untenable without a healthy lifestyle. A Healthy lifestyle comes from what we are nourished, exercise and hygiene. Students of Christ are those who always feed from Christ, practice spiritual life and live the life of holiness because they are saved.

Students of Christ died to sin and aspire to live a life that puts Christ as a priority. Music, culture, emotion, and violence of any kind whether in words or in actions never drag them from Christ. Music is not sin but our music needs to be guided by the word not emotion or not any secular situation. Emotions need to be controlled and redeemed.

Above all, the students of Christ are true believers that never compromise over the Lordship of Christ, their call to be students and the notion that they repudiated anything that may entangle them from walking with Christ. To be a student of Christ is to walk uninterruptedly, at any cost wherever and whenever. They are not situation driven; walk when life is conducive or not conducive. Every time is conducive! Every time is a time of learning. Students are always students and they are in studentship throughout their life. Amen.

Reference

Alford, D. L. (1967). *Music in the Pentecostal church*. Cleveland, TN: Pathway Press.

Anderson, T. L., & Skinner, S. A. (2019). Feelings: Discipleship that Understands the Affective Processes of a Disciple of Christ. *Christian Education Journal: Research on Educational Ministry, 16* (1), 66-78. doi:10.1177/0739891318820333

Arismawan, D. (2019). Ted Turner quotes about winners. Retrieved from https://quotescover.com/ted-turner-quote-about-winners.

Brasher, C. (2015, June 3). The Power of Music: For The Church. Retrieved August 17, 2020, from https://ftc.co/resource-library/blog-entries/the-power-of-music/

Bravery. The Positivity Project. (2016, July 6). https://posproject.org/p2-for-families/35/bravery/.

Bloomquist, J. (2010). Lying, cheating, and stealing: A study of categorical misdeeds. *Journal of Pragmatics, 42*(6), 1595–1605. doi: 10.1016/j.pragma.2009.11.008

Bonhoeffer, D. (1959). *The cost of discipleship*. London: SCM Press.

Bräutigam, M. (2019). Luther's Heidelberg Disputation and identity formation. *Dialog, 58*(1), 70–78. doi: 10.1111/dial.12455

Calenberg, R. D. (1981). *The New Testament doctrine of discipleship*. Place of publication not identified: Grace Theological Seminary.

Camp, L. (2008). *Mere discipleship: Radical Christianity in a rebellious world*. Grand Rapids, MI: Brazos Press.

Cane, A. (2017). *The place of Judas Iscariot in Christology*. London: Routledge.

Carr, A. (2003). *Is Jesus Calling You?* The Sermon Notebook/newtestament/ Mark. http://www.sermonnotebook.org/.

Click, E. D. (2000). *The inner circle: studying the lives of 13 apostles*. Lima, OH: CSS Pub. Co.

Carlson, S. (2010, March 7). "Characteristics of a True Disciple" March 7, 2010

Chester, T. (2020, July 21). SUFFERING FOLLOWED BY GLORY – THE PATTERN FOR DISCIPLES. Retrieved August 17, 2020, from https:// timchester.files.wordpress.com/

Chrispal, A. (2019, September). *International Orality Network | Restoring Missional Vision in Theological Education*. Https://Orality.Net/Content/ Restoring-Missional-Vision-in-Theological-Education/. https://orality. net/content/restoring-missional-vision-in-theological-education/

Chester, T. (2009). *The ordinary hero: living the cross and resurrection*. Nottingham: Inter-Varsity Press.

Celevier, E. (2020, September 22). *Does the promise have an expiration date?* Jesus.net. https://jesus.net/miracle/does-the-promise-have- an-expiration-date/.

Coster, G. T. (2011). *The Call of Elisha*. Bible Hub. https://biblehub.com/ sermons/auth/coster/the_call_of_elisha.htm

Cummings, G. (2008). *A study of the twelve apostles*. Okl: Tate Publishing.

Daft, R. L., & Lane, P. (2005). *Management* (14th ed.). South-Western Cengage Learning.

Davies, P. E. (1956). Trends toward Individualism in the Teaching of Jesus. *Journal of the American Academy of Religion, XXIV* (1), 10-17. doi:10.1093/jaarel/xxiv.1.10

Deffenbaugh, B. (2004, June 1). 15. Discipleship: Its Definitions and Dangers (Matthew 23:1-12). Retrieved August 14, 2020, from https://bible.org/seriespage/15-discipleship-its-definitions-and-dangers-matthew-231-12

Deines, R. (2014). Galilee and the Historical Jesus in Recent Research. Retrieved April 11, 2019, from http://www.augsburgfortress.org/media/downloads/9781451466744Chapt1excerpt.pdf

Eric Eve, The Jewish Context of Jesus' Miracles, (Sheffield: Sheffield Academic Press, 2002) Leicester, England: Inter-Varsity Press.

Faraoanu, I. (2015). The Call and Mission of the Disciple in the Gospel According to Mark. *International Letters of Social and Humanistic Sciences, 60,* 67–76. doi: 10.18052/www.scipress.com/ilshs.60.67

Farley, M. (2018). Risks of Prostitution: When the Person Is the Product. *Journal of the Association for Consumer Research,3*(1), 97-108. doi:10.1086/695670

France, R. T. (1976). *I came to set the earth on fire: a portrait of Jesus.* Downers Grove, IL: InterVarsity Pr.

Fiensy, D. A., & Strange, J. R. (2014). *Galilee in the late second temple and Mishnaic periods.* Minneapolis: Fortress

Garland, D. E. (1996). *Mark: From Biblical text-- to contemporary life.* Zondervan.

Gianotti, C. R.Gianotti (1999, p.16) September). *MIRACLES AND FAITH - Bible Equip.* https://bible-equip.org/articles/biblical-theological/Miracles.pdf.

Goffman, E. (1951). Symbols of Class Status. *The British Journal of Sociology,2*(4), 294.doi:10.2307/588083

GotQuestions.org. (2015, September 2). What is nominalism? Retrieved November 7, 2019, from https://www.gotquestions.org/nominalism.html.

Grannis, J. C., Laffin, A. J., &Schade, E. (1981). *The risk of the cross: Christian discipleship in the nuclear age.* New York: Seabury Press.

Greenwold, D. (2007). Being a First-Century Disciple. Retrieved April 12, 2018, from https://bible.org/article/being-first-century-disciple.

Guillebaud, S., &Guillebaud, S. (2011). *More than conquerors: a call to radical discipleship.* United States: Monarch Books.

Hays, R. (2012). Learning Leadership from Moses A Biblical Model for the Church Today, 1–48.

Hengel, M. (2005). *The charismatic leader and his followers.* Eugene, OR: Wipf& Stock.

Henrichsen, W. A., & Hendricks, H. G. (1988). *Disciples are made not born helping others grow to maturity in Christ.* Eastbourne, East Sussex: David C Cook.

Herrick, G. (2004, May 11). 3. Understanding The Theological Context of Biblical Discipleship. Retrieved August 14, 2020, from https://bible.org/seriespage/3-understanding-theological-context-biblical-discipleship

Hinks, D. (2003). The Bible's Definition of "Christian". Retrieved April 30, 2020, from https://www.journal33.org/disciple/pdf/christn.pdf

Houston, T. (1986). *Characters around the Cross.* First Edition edition: Marc Europe;.Europe.

Hubbard, M. (2014, February 25). "Let the One Who Has No Sword, Buy One": The Biblical Argument for Gun Control, Part Two. Retrieved March 18, 2020, from https://www.biola.edu/blogs/good-book-blog/2014/let-the-one-who-has-no-sword-buy-one-the-biblical-argument-for-gun-control-part-two

Ingram, P. E. (2017, November 3). *Diversity Discussion Starters.* Penn State Extension. https://extension.psu.edu/diversity-discussion-starters

Kelly, B. (2007). Simon Peter, the Man and His Ministry. Retrieved May 7, 2020, from http://www.stjohnlutheran-elyria.org/

Kern, M. (2001). THE APOSTLE JOHN The Beloved Apostle Perfecting the Love ... Retrieved August 16, 2020, from https://www.stathanasius.org/site/assets/files/1857/study_09_26_12.pdf pp. 886-903

Kim, S. S. (2010). *The miracles of Jesus according to John: their christological and eschatological significance.* Eugene, Or.:Wipf & Stock.

Kimball, S. W. (2006). *Lehren der Präsidenten der Kirche: Spencer W. Kimball.* Salt Lake City, UT: Intellectual Reserve.

Kinsella, E. L., Igou, E. R., & Ritchie, T. D. (2017). Heroism and the Pursuit of a Meaningful Life. *Journal of Humanistic Psychology,59*(4), 474-498. doi:10.1177/0022167817701002

Kolb, R. (1993). *The Christian faith: A Lutheran exposition.* St. Louis, MO: Concordia Pub. House.

Kretzschmar, L. (2013). THE GAP BETWEEN BELIEF AND ACTION: WHY IS IT THAr CHRISTIANS DO NOT PRACTISE WHAT THEY PREACH? *Scriptura, 62*(0), 311-321. doi: 10.7833/62-0-624

Laurie, G. (2019, October 5). God's promises: No expiration date. Retrieved December 9, 2019, from https://www.wnd.com/2019/10/gods-promises-no-expiration-date/

Lazar, S. (2019). Cheap Law or Cheap Grace? Dietrich Bonhoeffer and Gerhard Forde on the Nature of Law and Gospel. Retrieved December 9, 2019, from https://www.academia.edu/5300005/Cheap_Law_or_Cheap_Grace_Dietrich_Bonhoeffer_and_Gerhard_Forde_on_the_Nature_of_Law_and_Gospel.

Lim, D. (2017, September 01). TAKE UP YOUR CROSS AND FOLLOW ME. Retrieved August 17, 2020, from http://www.ololbayswater.org.au/newsletters/2017/9/2/22nd-sunday-in-ordinary-time-a-3rd-september-2017

Longman, T. (2010). Christianity and Genocide in Rwanda. *Christianity and Genocide in Rwanda*, Xv-Xvi. doi:10.1017/cbo9780511642043.001

Lucas, R. C., & Green, C. (1995). *The message of 2 Peter & Jude: the promise of His coming.*

McBirnie, W. S. (2008). *The search for the twelve apostles.* Wheaton, IL: Tyndale House.

MacArthur, J. (2002). *Twelve ordinary men: how the Master shaped his disciples for greatness, and what He wants to do with you.* Nashville, TN: Thomas Nelson.

MacArthur, J. (2003). *The keys to spiritual growth: Unlocking the riches of God.* Vereeniging: Christian Art.

MacDonald, J. A. (2010). Retrieved November 7, 2010, from https://biblehub.com/sermons/auth/macdonald/the_call_of_elisha.htm.

Măcelaru, M. (2001). Discipleship in the Old Testament and Its Context: A Phenomenological Approach. Retrieved August 14, 2020, from https://www.academia.edu/3811502/Discipleship_in_the_Old_Testament_and_Its_Context_A_Phenomenological_Approach, pp. 11-22

McCasland, D. (2016, February 23). ODB: The Power of God's Music. Retrieved August 17, 2020, from https://ymi.today/2016/03/odb-the-power-of-gods-music/

McGrath, A. (1988). Justification by Faith. Grand Rapids, MI: Académie Books.

Meier, J. P. (1997). The Circle of the Twelve: Did It Exist during Jesus' Public Ministry? *Journal of Biblical Literature, 116*(4), 635. https://doi.org/10.2307/3266551

Meisinger, G. (2004, May 26). Judas. Retrieved August 17, 2020, from https://bible.org/article/judas

Menzies, M. (2015, February 5). Christianity. Retrieved August 13, 2020, from https://rlp.hds.harvard.edu/files/hds-rlp/files/christianity.pdf

Merchant, N. (2017). *The power of onlyness: How to make your ideas mighty enough to dent the world*. New York: Viking.

Mattes, M. (2012). Discipleship in Lutheran Perspective - Lutheran Quarterly. Retrieved November 22, 2019, from http://www.lutheranquarterly.com/uploads/7/4/0/1/7401289/26-2-mattes.pdf.

Merriam Webster Dictionary. (2019). Imitate. Retrieved December 15, 2019, from https://www.merriam-webster.com/dictionary/imitate..

Meyer, J. (2008). *Never give up!: relentless determination to overcome life's challenges*. Nashville, Tennessee: Faith words.

Miiller, D. 1975. μαθητής. In The new international dictionary of New Testament theology. Edited by Colin Brown. Grand Rapids, MI: Zondervan Publishing House.

Mitchell, M. (2020, August 13). The role of faith in emotions: A pastoral study / Marika ... Retrieved August 13, 2020, from https://core.ac.uk/display/38215557

Moffic, R. (2014). 20 Things You Can Learn About Leadership From Moses. Retrieved August 15, 2020, from http://www.yfc.net/images/uploads/general/20-tips-from-moses.pdf

Nolland, J. (2005). *The Gospel of Matthew: A commentary on the Greek text*. Bletchley, Milton Keynes: Paternoster Press.

Ogden, G. (2016). *Transforming discipleship: Making disciples a few at a time*. Downers Grove, IL: IVP Books, an imprint of InterVarsity Press.

Ogden, G. (2003). *Transforming discipleship: making disciples a few at a time*. Downers Grove, IL: IVP Books, an imprint of InterVarsity Press.

Onyinah, O. (2017). The Meaning of Discipleship. *International Review of Mission*, *106*(2), 216–227. https://doi.org/10.1111/irom.12181

Otokola, E. O. (2017, September 30). *The Importance of Theological Education to the Changing World*. Zenodo. https://zenodo.org/record/1036646#.XwzjjShKjIU

Parker, P. (1962). John the son of Zebedee and the Fourth Gospel. *Journal of Biblical Literature, 81*(1), 35. https://doi.org/10.2307/3264824

Perrett, R. W. (2013). *Death and immortality.* Springer Science & Business Media. doi: Volume 10 of Studies in Philosophy and Religion

PORTER, E. D. U. A. R. D. O. (2013, June 13). https://economix.blogs. nytimes.com/2013/06/13/how-money-affects-morality/. *How Money Affects Morality.* Retrieved from https://economix.blogs.nytimes. com/2013/06/13/how-money-affects-morality/

Rowling, J. K. (1998). *Harry Potter and the chamber of secrets.* London: Bloomsbury.

Schoenheit, J. W. (2015). *The Calling of the Disciples.* Http:// Thesowermagazine.Com/the-Calling-of-the-Disciples/. http:// thesowermagazine.com/the-calling-of-the-disciples/

Shirley, C. (2008, November 2). It Takes a Church to Make a Disciple: An Integrative Model of Discipleship for the Local Church. South West Journal of Theology. (Volume 50), 208-224.

Simpson, A. (2015). Cross of Christ) 3. THE BRAND OF THE CROSS. Retrieved August 17, 2020, from http://www.sermonindex.net/ modules/articles/index.php?view=article

Smith, D. M. (1995). The theology of the "Gospel of John". Cambridge: Cambridge University Press.

Snape, H. (1971). Peter and Paul in Rome. *The Modern Churchman, 14*(2), 127–138. doi: 10.3828/mc.14.2.127

Strode, Tom. (2016). *WRAP-UP: ERLC event addresses culture, Gospel.* Baptist Press. https://www.baptistpress.com/resource-library/news/ wrap-up-erlc-event-addresses-culture-gospel/

Tarrants, T. (2014). Why Every Christian Is a Disciple. Retrieved August 17, 2020, from https://www.christianpost.com/news/why-every-christian-is-a-disciple.html

Tommy, S. (2004), THE DISCIPLES' FAILURE. http://www.biblecourses. com/English/en lessons/EN 199101 08.pdf

Waite, J. (2010). The Desponding Prophet. Retrieved August 18, 2020, from https://biblehub.com/sermons/auth/waite/the_desponding_prophet.htm

Wilkins, M. J. (2004). *Matthew*. Grand Rapids, MI: Zondervan..

WHITAKER, R. O. B. Y. N. (2013, October). Rebuke or Recall? Rethinking the Role of Peter in Mark's ... Retrieved March 21, 2020, from https://repository.divinity.edu.au/2020/1/Rebuke and Recall CBQ.pdf

Willington, H. (1999). Character Profile: Matthew (disciple). Retrieved April 8, 2020, from https://www.historicjesus.com/character/matthew. html

04089948-00835882

Printed in the United States
by Baker & Taylor Publisher Services